Garnie A. Brand, State Secretary
Baptist Training Union
291 Peachtree St., N. E.
Atlanta, Georgia   30303

A Church
Training Adults

ROBERT S. COOK

Convention Press

NASHVILLE **TENNESSEE**

© 1966 • CONVENTION PRESS
Nashville, Tennessee

5118-13

To my wife

HELEN

Who has proved the concepts of this book,
in theory and practice,
as the most dedicated, inspiring, and competent
Adult union leader
whom the author has known

Code Number: Church Study Course
This book is number 1813 in category 18,
section for Adults and Young People

Library of Congress Catalog Card Number: 66-13314
Printed in the United States of America

50. D 65 R.R.D.

About the Author

ROBERT S. COOK is consultant for adult work, field services section, Training Union Department, Baptist Sunday School Board, Nashville, Tennessee.

Dr. Cook was born in West, Texas, September 1, 1924. Reared in an active Baptist home, his first memories of church life are of attending meetings led by one of his dedicated parents. His deacon father was especially active as Training Union director both in his church and in the association.

Converted at nine years of age at a Royal Ambassador camp, Dr. Cook was baptized at ten into the First Baptist Church, Hillsboro, Texas. In 1943, the Cooks joined other war-moving families in First Baptist Church, Grand Prairie, Texas.

During World War II, Dr. Cook served with an artillery unit in several major European theater campaigns.

Dr. Cook is a graduate of Baylor University, Waco, Texas, and of Southwestern Baptist Theological Seminary, Fort Worth, Texas, from which he received a master's degree and, in 1958, a doctor's degree in religious education. He has attended Utah State University and has done special graduate study at both the University of Tennessee and George Peabody College for Teachers, Nashville, Tennessee.

Dr. Cook has served in various positions of Training Union leadership in the churches where he has held membership. Prior to joining the Training Union Department of the Baptist Sunday School Board in July, 1952, he was minister of education and music at Saginaw Baptist Church, Fort Worth, Texas.

He is married to the former Eva Helen Mills. The Cooks have two children, Randall Mills and Barbara Helen.

Preface

GOD HAS BLESSED Southern Baptists with the privilege of accomplishing much in this generation. In this there is rejoicing and prayer that his blessing for service may continue as this group is found fit for his purpose.

A specter looms over this denomination, however—the sight of what could have been done if there had been more than half the members in active service through their churches.

The writer believes that this tremendous number of inactive church members is composed primarily of redeemed persons who love the Lord. He is of the opinion that this lack of active participation and service is due to failure on the part of churches to properly interpret to the members the responsibilities of church membership and to train them in how to fulfil these tasks in a satisfying manner.

What could be done if all churches were to recognize this obligation and devote a major portion of their interests and resources in adequately "building up the saved" for service? This exciting vision became the call which brought the writer to the directorship of Training Union work for Adults in 1952. The call has remained strong, the conviction of the need has deepened, and the vision of what can be done in service for Christ by adults through their churches has grown clearer.

Increased and improved resources are now available for this work because of the enlarged editorial staff. John A. Ishee, editor of adult materials, is supported by two former editors, Raymond M. Rigdon and LeRoy Ford, now in supervisory positions; and aided by Mrs. Louise Ellerker, assistant editor, and Mrs. Ruby McMillin, editorial assistant.

An enlarged program of Training Union work in churches and in the denomination is being introduced with new tasks, new content areas of study, and new quarterly training guides for leaders and adults in church member training.

To present these new and enlarged concepts of a training program for all adult church members, and to describe the materials and methods for accomplishing them, required the preparation of this new text. (A Glossary of new terms and concepts is included on pp. 151 ff.) This text replaces *The Baptist Adult Union Manual*, by J. E. Lambdin, in Category 18 of the Church Study Course. The writer acknowledges an unmeasured personal and denominational debt to this pioneer religious educator. In this book the writer has attempted to retain and build on the basic principles for training adult church members which Dr. Lambdin conceived and developed for Southern Baptists during his more than thirty-five years of service.

A heavy debt is owed to Roger Skelton, supervisor of the Training Union department Adult-Youth field services section, for encouragement and help in revising drafts of the manuscript. A special tribute is offered to Mrs. J. E. Lambdin for her encouraging review of the first manuscript.

Upon the occasion of their Golden Wedding Anniversary in 1997, the undersigned will not have finished thanking his wife, who for three hectic months had no social or personal life—only the administration of her household of two active children around the clutter of stacks of notated resources, writing materials, and bits of manuscript. Her invaluable aid in checking research sources, typing the roughest of the manuscript corrections, and preparing the "Questions for Review and Written Work" can never be adequately compensated. Hers has been an expression of joint dedication, and can only be warmly admired and affectionately appreciated.

ROBERT S. COOK

Contents

Church Study Course

THE CHURCH STUDY COURSE began October 1, 1959. It is a merger of three courses previously promoted by the Sunday School Board—the Sunday School Training Course, the Graded Training Union Study Course, and the Church Music Training Course. On October 1, 1961, the Woman's Missionary Union principles and methods studies were added.

The course is fully graded. The system of awards provides a series of five diplomas of twenty books each for Adults or Young People, two diplomas of five books each for Intermediates and for Juniors.

The course is comprehensive, with books grouped into twenty categories. The purpose of the course is to help Christians to grow in knowledge and conviction, to help them to grow toward maturity in Christian character and competence for service, to encourage them to participate worthily as workers in their churches, and to develop leaders for all phases of church life and work.

The Church Study Course is promoted by the Baptist Sunday School Board, 127 Ninth Avenue, North, Nashville, Tennessee 37203, through its Sunday School, Training Union, Church Music, and Church Administration Departments; and the Woman's Missionary Union, 600 North Twentieth Street, Birmingham, Alabama 35203; and by the respective departments in the states affiliated with the Southern Baptist Convention. A description of the course and the system of awards may be found in the leaflet "Trained Workmen," which may be obtained without charge from any one of these departments named.

A record of all awards earned should be maintained in each church. A person should be designated by the church to keep the files. Forms for such records may be ordered from any Baptist Book Store.

Requirements for Credit in Class
or Home Study

If CREDIT is desired for the study of this book in a class or by home study the following requirements must be met:

I. In Classwork

1. The class must meet a minimum of seven and one-half clock hours. The required time does not include assembly periods. Ten class periods of forty-five minutes each are recommended. (If laboratory or clinical work is desired in specialized or technical courses, this requirement may be met by six clock hours of classwork and three clock hours of supervised laboratory or clinical work.)

2. A class member who attends all class sessions and completes the reading of the book within a week following the last class session will not be required to do any written work.

3. A class member who is absent from one or more sessions must answer the questions on all chapters he misses. In such a case, he must turn in his paper within a week, and he must certify that he has read the book.

4. The teacher should request an award for himself.

5. The teacher should complete the "Request for Book Awards —Class Study" (Form 150) and forward it within two weeks after the completion of the class to the Church Study Course Awards Office, 127 Ninth Avenue, North, Nashville, Tennessee 37203.

II. In home Study

1. A person who does not attend any class session may receive credit by answering all questions for written work as indicated in the book. When a person turns in his paper on home study, he must certify that he has read the book.

2. Students may find profit in studying the text together, but

individual papers are required. Carbon copies or duplicates in any form cannot be accepted.

3. Home study work papers may be graded by the pastor or a person designated by him, or they may be sent to the Church Study Course Awards Office for grading. The form entitled "Request for Book Awards—Home Study" (Form 151) must be used in requesting awards. It should be mailed to Church Study Course Awards Office, 127 Ninth Avenue, North, Nashville, Tennessee 37203.

III. CREDIT FOR THIS BOOK

This book is number 1813 in category 18, section for Adults and Young People.

CHAPTER 1

1

The Right Concept
of a Church Is Essential

ADULT CHURCH MEMBERS constitute the greatest hope for churches in accomplishing their work for Christ in the world today. The work of a church requires trained members. No other group of persons needs training more than adults; no other persons can do more than trained adults.

Adults in training to do effective work in their churches need first to understand what a church is. All programs of training and methods of service must be true to a proper concept of a church. They must find their foundation and direction at this point. So adults, in studying the training program of their church, must begin with an investigation of a church—its nature, its purpose, and its functions.

Living creatures generally defy simple definitions formed into comprehensive yet concise statements. So it is that acceptable definitions of a church are not easily stated. How can one define a personality? Such a living body, reflecting so vividly the power-filled person of its founder, seems to demand several volumes for adequate description. Yet, this relatively short text, in properly dealing first with an understanding of a church, must define it as a basic concept.

Three brief statements from representative sources are here combined to offer a satisfactory descriptive definition for the purpose of this study.

"A New Testament church . . . is a local body of baptized believers who are associated by a covenant in the faith and

---

[1] *Book of Reports* (Nashville: Southern Baptist Convention Executive Committee, 1963), p. 183. Used by permission.

fellowship of the gospel";[1] it is "founded by Christ for the purpose of spreading his kingdom on earth." [2] "The church is by nature both a spiritual fellowship and a functioning institution." [3]

A church is an *organism*—a living creation of God, empowered by him to do his work in the world. The essential character or nature of a church requires that it act or *function* by certain characteristic expressions to achieve a God-given purpose. The *basic continuing activities* by which a church moves toward its purpose are known as *tasks*. Engaging in these activities requires the relating of church members through organization to accomplish the tasks of their church. The adult must find and understand his related place and responsibility in this organism.

At least 84 times out of 114 the word "church" is used in the New Testament in its local sense—referring to a local congregation. (See Matt. 18:17; Acts 14:23; Rom. 16:5; 1 Cor. 4:17; Col. 4:15; 1 Thess. 1:1; et.al.) "Church" is treated in that sense in this book, which is written to describe a church's training program. This program is designed for use in a church—a body composed of regenerate persons in Christ who have given public profession of their faith by baptism and have voluntarily banded themselves together to grow and serve in the fellowship of a local congregation.

I. A Church as an Organism

A church is a living thing. It is vibrantly alive, sustained by the life of the resurrected Christ and empowered by the ever-present Holy Spirit. As an organism, a church is made up of redeemed members in relationship. It has a nature, a purpose, and certain functions.

1. *The Nature of a Church*

The nature of a church can be related to the triune God.

---

[2] H. W. Tribble, *Our Doctrines* (Nashville: Convention Press, 1936), p. 107. Used by permission.

[3] Franklin M. Segler, *A Theology of Church and Ministry* (Nashville: Broadman Press, 1960) p. 11.

1. *God.*—A church may be properly described as *the family of God.* Redeemed persons who make up a church are referred to throughout the New Testament as "sons of God." (See John 1:12; Rom. 8:14; Gal. 4:7; Phil. 2:15; and 1 John 3:1.) Members are also referred to as "children of God" (Matt. 5:9; Luke 20:36; Rom. 8:16; 1 John 3:10) and "heirs of God" (Rom. 8:17; Gal. 3:29; Titus 3:7).

2. *Christ.*—A church is also described in the Bible as *the body of Christ.* This figure indicates that all members share Christ by having put on Christ and by having been incorporated into Christ. They all live together under Christ as the head (Eph. 4:15), having union with him and with one another in him. Indeed, all members who are members of Christ are members also of one another. (See 1 Cor. 12; Rom. 12; and Eph. 1:23; 4:4,12.)

3. *Holy Spirit.*—A church is also known as the *community of the Holy Spirit.* This emphasis characterizes the churches described in the book of Acts. Members who were related in a rather insignificant group, which was not particularly distinctive from any other social group, became transformed by the infilling of the Holy Spirit to become a "fellowship of the Spirit" (Phil. 2:1) and to be given power for accomplishing the work of Christ in the world. (See Acts 1:8; 8:17; 19:6; Rom. 8:9,11,14; 1 Cor. 3:16; 2 Cor. 13:14.) The Holy Spirit guides churches in selecting leaders (Acts 13:2) and directs and challenges them in their work.

Perhaps the most vivid figure used to describe a church is that of the body of Christ. This figure suggests a living organism with many essential members. A church is organized like a body; it is a body characterized by *fellowship.* In it, people are bound together by a common experience and for a common purpose.

In the New Testament the key word used for fellowship is *koinonia.* This "fellowship or *koinonia* signifies a common participation, a togetherness, a community life." [4] It has its

---

[4] From *The Misunderstanding of the Church,* Emil Brunner. Tr. Harold Knight. Copyright 1953, W. L. Jenkins. The Westminster Press. Used by permission.

basis in the common experience of personal faith and commitment to Christ and continues in a church in the presence of the Holy Spirit. In the first New Testament church, conditions described indicate various areas in which this fellowship was exercised (Acts 2:41–47). John spoke of having "fellowship one with another" (1 John 1:7). Other New Testament writers referred to members of a church as "fellowheirs" (Eph. 3:6) and "fellowcitizens" (Eph. 2:19); "fellowservant" (Col. 1:7). These terms are joined by those further indicating fellowship as service in Christ's body: "fellowworker" (Col. 4:11); "fellowhelpers" (3 John 8); and "fellowheirs" (Eph. 3:6).

2. The Purpose of a Church

Churches were founded to accomplish the work of Christ. A clue to a church's purpose is expressed succinctly in Ephesians: " . . . for the equipping of the saints for the work of service, to the building up of the body of Christ; until we all attain to the unity of the faith, and of the knowledge of the Son of God, to a mature man, to the measure of the stature which belongs to the fullness of Christ (Eph. 4:12–13, NASB).[5]

Churches are established in order to glorify God and to minister to the needs of their members. They are also to continue to find the unsaved; attempt to reach them with the good news of the redeeming work of Christ; and lead them to a commitment to his lordship and service.

The church thus becomes the agency of saved people for enabling them to 'grow in grace and in the knowledge of our Lord and Saviour Jesus Christ'; and, combining with one another, most effectively to bear witness to salvation, in the most extensive measure possible.[6]

---

[5] *New American Standard Bible, New Testament,* © The Lockman Foundation, 1960, 1962, 1963.

[6] William Owen Carver, *The Furtherance of the Gospel* (Nashville: The Sunday School Board of the Southern Baptist Convention, 1935), p. 57. Used by permission.

3. *The Functions of a Church*

An organism has characteristic functions. Inherent in the nature and purpose of a church is the work it is to do. The scope of the work of a church is its characteristic functions.

The basic functions of a church are to worship, to witness, to learn, and to minister.

(1) *To worship is to experience an awareness of God, to recognize his holiness and majesty, and to respond in loving obedience to his leadership.* Worship is the primary function of a church since it must come first and the other functions are dependent upon it.

Regular worship, both private and corporate, is most important in the life of Christians today. True worship helps a man to maintain his identity with God; fulfils a need for fellowship with fellow believers; gives understanding and purpose to life; helps to show answers to problems; gives strength for living fully; and helps a man to live above finite limitations through the power of God. True worship should result in service to the Lord Christ and in witness to him in the world.

One of Southern Baptists' most outstanding and practical theologians, W. T. Conner, has written that worship of God in Christ is the primary function of a church. "The first business, then, of a church is not evangelism, nor missions, nor benevolence"; he stated, "it is worship." [7]

(2) *To witness is to declare what God has done in and through Jesus Christ for the salvation of men.*

Every church member is to witness, both by the way he lives his life as a consistent Christian and the way he shares his testimony concerning how Christ saved him and how he can do as much for them. Witnessing is an act of service which should result from a church member's engaging in the function of worship. "Ye shall be witnesses unto me" (Acts 1:8).

---

[7] W. T. Conner, *The Gospel of Redemption* (Nashville: Broadman Press, 1945), p. 277.

(3) *To learn is to grow in understanding, form new attitudes, and develop actions consistent with the example of Christ.* The function of helping church members to learn in the Christian life is a continuous and essential action growing out of the nature and purpose of a church.

Learning includes both teaching and training. The process never truly ends, for Christian growth is never complete. The objective is, "So that the man of God may be complete and proficient, well-fitted and thoroughly equipped for every good work" (2 Tim. 3:17, *The Amplified New Testament*)[8] and so that he "may grow up into him in all things, which is the head, even Christ" (Eph. 4:15). Paul advised, "Study to shew thyself approved unto God, a workman that needeth not to be ashamed, rightly dividing the word of truth" (2 Tim. 2:15). And Peter admonished, "Be ready always to give an answer to every man that asketh you a reason of the hope that is in you" (1 Peter 3:15).

(4) *To minister is to make a loving response to the needs of persons in Jesus' name.*

The things that characterize the life and work of Christ should characterize church members. They should minister to all men. Jesus said, "Whosoever will be great among you, let him be your minister; . . . even as the Son of man came not to be ministered unto, but to minister, and to give his life a ransom for many" (Matt. 20:26–28).

This function of the church is not restricted to the pastor or to the other "ministers" of a church staff. Every church member should be concerned with ministering one to another. These actions which reveal the love of Christ are an expression of the basic nature of the church as a fellowship.

Acts of ministry are critically needed in these days. People seem to have more troubles than ever before. As churches become larger and members can receive proportionately less of the pastor's time in acts of ministry, the blessed opportu-

---

[8] The quotations in this book from *The Amplified New Testament* were copyrighted in 1958 by the Lockman Foundation, LaHabra, California. Used by permission.

nities for visiting the sick, helping the needy, lifting up the fallen, encouraging the discouraged, and sharing "a cup of cold water in . . . [Jesus'] name" generally become more acute. These ministries may be more effective when performed by fellow members of the congregation. It cannot be suggested of them that they perform these ministries because it is their vocation.

4. The Tasks of a Church

Action is involved when any organism functions. When a church functions as an organism, there are jobs to be done. Some of these jobs are basic responsibilities which demand continuing action. Such actions are called *tasks*. When a church carries out its tasks, it accomplishes the purposes for which it was created. The method of accomplishing tasks may vary among churches, but essentially the same tasks have been carried on since churches were established by Christ.

Church tasks may be found by studying the New Testament. It would be a most profitable exercise for every congregation to gather itself in a fellowship of investigative study, New Testaments in hand, and seek to set down the tasks which they understand Christ to have assigned their congregation. It would be profitable, perhaps at the outset of such a study, for the congregation to determine from these sources what its true objectives are. Then any basic continuing activity that has primary importance in moving toward these objectives would be considered a task.

Some tasks which a church would likely discover are: to preach to believers and unbelievers; to lead its members to worship, witness, learn and minister; to teach its constituents the biblical revelation, systematic theology, Christian ethics, Christian history, and Baptist polity and organization; to perform church functions; to learn about and become involved in missions; to develop skills in singing, leading and playing music; to reach all prospects for the church; to orient all church members; and to send persons and gifts to bring all men of all nations to Christ.

A church by its nature has a co-mission with Christ; it also has a commission from Christ: "Go ye therefore, and teach all nations, baptizing them in the name of the Father, and of the Son, and of the Holy Ghost; teaching them to observe all things whatsoever I have commanded you: and, lo, I am with you alway, even unto the end of the world" (Matt. 28:19–20).

II. A CHURCH AS AN ORGANIZATION

1. Concept of Organization

In the halls, councils, and chat-sessions of Baptist churches, well-intentioned persons may have made statements similar to the following: "What's wrong with us is, we have too much organization. If we could get rid of so much organization around here, and just let the Holy Spirit take charge and lead us, we would be better off."

Certainly, no one would take issue with that part of the statement which suggests that the Holy Spirit should be the leader and guide for all that we do in our churches. Many of the problems which we experience could be avoided if his leadership were followed.

A statement, however, which suggests that organization and spirituality are contrary to each other needs to be challenged. Regarding organization as unspiritual is hardly in keeping either with the purposes of organization, with its use in accomplishing spiritual objectives in churches today, or with examples of its use as recorded in the Bible.

Examples of the utilization of organization in spiritual undertakings abound throughout the Scriptures. Moses organized the children of Israel into units of thousands, hundreds, and tens in order that they might be effectively governed and led to work together toward God's goal of the Promised Land (Ex. 18:13–27). God outlined a very complex system of *organization* when he described the design of the tabernacle, its contents, and the activities which should occur there (Ex. 25:1 to 31:18). The Temple was later built to this design. Also the titles and explicit job descriptions of Temple officers as well as the specific functions which were to be engaged upon in certain areas were set forth.

The New Testament shows that Jesus used organization. He *organized* his followers or disciples with the purpose of teaching and training them so that they could be sent to carry out his objectives. (See Matt. 10:5–8.) For example, there was the organization of the twelve, the seventy, and the one hundred twenty. Jesus sent them two by two, instructing them to go and put into practice the things which they had learned. They were then to return and report the results of their efforts. This process was pedagogically sound. It utilized *organization* as a vehicle in the learning process. It is copied to a striking degree today in much of the organized work of the churches in carrying out Christ's objectives.

The first chapters of Acts record what is considered to be one of the most "spiritual" occasions in the biblical account—the coming of the Holy Spirit at Pentecost. The passage describes how the apostles gathered in an upper room where they were of one accord. There they prayed, waited on the Lord, and perhaps engaged in other spiritual exercises.

The Acts account also relates that the apostles were engaged in something which could be considered by some as being very "unspiritual." *They were perfecting their organization.* It is recorded in considerable detail how they selected one to "be ordained to be a witness with us of his resurrection. . . . That he may take part of this ministry and apostleship, from which Judas by transgression fell" (Acts 1:22–25). The next chapter of the book then tells how the one who was thus elected stood with the others on the day of Pentecost, serving and being used mightily by the Lord. There seemed to have been jobs for each of the twelve that day; each was functioning in the capacity which God had planned for him and assigned to him.

Organization was used by the early churches as they assigned certain ministries to designated offices (Acts 6:1–7). Organization is described further in the New Testament in Paul's classic figure of a church likened to the human body with its members organized to work together in their different ways to carry out the purposes of God (1 Cor. 12:13–14).

Organization is a spiritual tool; organization is also an educational tool. After a congregation has identified its essential tasks, it assigns these tasks to persons with skills and assists them in carrying out these tasks. Wise churches will seek to relate members in such a way as to use the power which is present in the person of the Holy Spirit in the most effective manner. Such arrangement is called *organization.*

Simply stated, *organization, as conceived and practiced in a church, is members arranging themselves in the best position possible to be used effectively by the Holy Spirit, working together toward accomplishing the objectives of their church.*

2. Tasks of Church Program Organizations

After a church has established its programs and organizations to conduct them, it is ready to plan its work. Efficient planning will require that *tasks* be grouped to become *programs.* Then these programs should be assigned to organizations to conduct. The traditional church program organizations are: Sunday School, Training Union, Brotherhood, Woman's Missionary Union, and Music Ministry. When assigned by the church, the task statements relate properly along the lines shown on the chart which appears on the next page.

3. Program Service Tasks

Program services are so designated because they serve other programs. The services which they provide greatly enrich the work of those other programs and make a positive contribution to the life of the entire congregation. The church library, audio-visual education, and church recreation are classified as program services.

(1) *Church library.*—A spiritual democracy, as practiced in Baptist churches, demands an informed membership. The genius of Baptist congregational life, and its cooperative

CHURCH TASKS PERFORMED BY SUNDAY SCHOOL, TRAINING UNION, WOMAN'S MISSIONARY UNION, BROTHERHOOD, AND MUSIC MINISTRY

For Evangelism, Missions, Stewardship, and Other Work of the Church

	Sunday School	Woman's Missionary Union	Brotherhood	Training Union	Music Ministry
Teaching	Teach the biblical revelation	Teach missions	Teach missions	Interpret systematic theology, Christian history, Christian ethics, and church polity and organization	Teach music and hymnody
Outreach	Reach all prospects for the church	Lead persons to participate in missions	Lead all men, young men, and boys to participate in mission activities	Give orientation to new church members	Lead all persons to participate in hymn singing
Performance of Functions	Lead all church members to worship, witness, learn, and minister daily			Train in performance of functions of the church	Assist the church in its functions of worship, proclamation, education, and ministry
Training				Discover, recruit, and train potential leaders	Train persons to lead, sing, and play music
Special Projects	Provide organization and leadership for special projects of the church—church budgets, revival meetings, special mission offerings, and other projects				
Channeling	Provide and interpret information (to the masses) regarding the work of the church and denomination				

effort in the denomination, is that every member of every congregation can *know* for himself.

In the search for truth, a church library is a vital service to all the church. It is a church's resource center. The church library is the means through which a church procures materials, cares for them, encourages their use, and circulates them to the people of the church. Included in this resource center for the church are printed materials, such as books, pamphlets, tracts, and clippings; audio-visual materials, such as slides, filmstrips, maps, pictures; and other learning aids and curriculum supplements. Audio-visual equipment and materials for displays, etc., are other resources which may be found in a church library.

(2) *Audio-visual education.*—Jesus used visual aids in his teaching. However, it is only in the memory of the present generation of church leaders that audio-visuals have been produced, made available, and used extensively by Baptists. These learning aids can be of great benefit. Educators have proved that such materials can assist pupils to learn faster, better, and more.

The audio-visual program service should (1) help church leaders plan to use these materials; (2) inform workers concerning available materials and equipment; (3) train leaders throughout the church to use the materials and equipment effectively.

(3) *Church recreation.*—Jesus was concerned with the physical needs of men. He frequently led his disciples away from service opportunities for rest. Jesus also spent much of his ministry in healing the bodies and minds of men. Baptist churches need to concern themselves with the recreational needs of their members. Persons in this day need help in learning how to relax from the strain of daily work and how to use properly their increased time away from the job.

Basically, church recreation provides another fruitful means of Christian fellowship. Congregations need relaxed opportunities through which to develop friendships, such as social activities, sports, retreats, and the like.

Church recreation program service should (1) determine

the kinds of recreation needed; (2) plan a program to include these activities; (3) assist the program organizations in recreational activities; and (4) develop leaders who can secure proper materials and help provide recreational service throughout the church. The coeducational feature of Training Union makes it the logical program organization to provide leadership in the church's social life.

4. *Administrative Service Tasks*

Administrative service tasks are performed by the pastor, church staff, deacons, nominating committee, personnel committee, and other church committees and officers. A church, as an organization, must be administered. Administration is a spiritual task; administration means "ministering to." Organization requires spiritual administration.

SUMMARY

A church as an organism indicates the way in which it should organize itself. The church as an organism must be organized. If it has proper organization, it will function.

Before a church organizes for spiritual endeavor, it should first understand its nature, purpose, and functions. This knowledge is basic as it then determines appropriate actions necessary to accomplish its work. Tasks should be stated, grouped into programs, and assigned to the appropriate organizations to be conducted for the church.

CHAPTER 2

I. THE TASKS OF THE TRAINING UNION PROGRAM
   1. Teach Systematic Theology, Christian Ethics, Christian History, and Church Polity and Organization
   2. Give Orientation to New Church Members
   3. Train All Church Members to Worship, Witness, Learn, and Minister Daily
   4. Train Leaders for the Church and the Denomination
   5. Provide Organization and Leadership for Special Projects of the Church
   6. Provide and Interpret Information Regarding the Work of the Church and the Denomination

II. RELATING TRAINING TO ADULT CHURCH MEMBERS
   1. Concept of Adulthood
   2. The Adult as a Church Recruit
   3. What a Church Promises the Adult Member
   4. What an Adult Member Promises His Church

2

A Church Training Program
for Adults Is Offered

OBSERVING THE PROGRESSION implied in the title, A CHURCH
TRAINING ADULTS, this book has presented first a church defined and described as an organism and as an organization.
Now comes a look at the *training program* of a church and
at the age group with which this book is concerned, *adults*.

Recall that in chapter 1, it was shown that a church should
state its basic tasks; group these tasks into programs; organize itself to conduct these programs; and assign its programs to the organizations established. In this chapter
attention will be given first to the *training* tasks which make
up the Training Union program of a church.

One principle of education is to provide a laboratory in
which individuals may enlarge upon the learning opportunities of the classroom.

Practice proves theory as well as provides for the development
of skills. As a matter of fact, theory is simply an idea, a figment
of the mind, until it has been proved in practice.[1]

*Training is educating in knowledge and skills through
study and practice.*

Training suggests a concern with skills. Skills may be
called the tools which a person needs to perform certain
actions that will lead toward the intended goals. However,
skills are not easily acquired. They cannot necessarily be
learned by going through certain motions (even under super-

---

[1] Harold K. Graves, *The Nature and Functions of a Church* (Nashville: Convention Press, 1963), p. 88. Used by permission.

vision) a sufficient number of times to make them become a conditioned response or habit. Matthew B. Miles, a leading authority in the field of education, has said: "Skillfulness is thus a complex integration of sensitivity, diagnostic ability and action." He goes on to amplify the point:

While the hope for simple techniques and magic panaceas is a natural one, effective training must be broadly based. Although training does deal with specific problems . . . recipes and prescriptions cannot be substituted for the learner's ability. . . .

Such skills as these are not motor skills, like those which the operator of a punch press has, nor are they conditioned responses or rote learning skills, like a dog's tricks. They are complex—but focused integrations of understanding, attitudes, and behavior.[2]

Miles has defined training in a restricted sense as "a planned way to practice and improve what one is doing or needs to do in the future."[3]

The word "training" also means "to bring to a requisite standard, as of knowledge or skill," and "to give education by instruction and discipline."[4]

Training in churches is done by guiding members in understanding needed concepts and in practicing their tasks sufficiently to become skilful when accomplishing them.

"The Training Union is the church's organization for training church members and leaders to perform the work of a church skilfully."[5]

The Training Union program provides the laboratory in which church members and leaders may develop skills by practicing church tasks. This training is not focused on de-

---

[2] Matthew B. Miles, *Learning to Work in Groups, A Program Guide for Educational Leaders* (New York: Bureau of Publications, Teachers College, Columbia University, 1959), pp. 32-33. Used by permission.

[3] *Ibid.*, p. 31. Used by permission.

[4] *The Desk Standard Dictionary* (New York: Funk & Wagnalls Company, 1946), p. 814.

[5] W. L. Howse, "The Training Concept in Training Union," (paper reported to Training Union Department, Baptist Sunday School Board, March 17, 1965), p. 1.

veloping individual skills alone. The major training emphasis in a church must be on team performance in order that the church may be able to accomplish its work effectively. No other church program is as dedicated to team effort as is the Training Union with its emphasis upon developing skills in group action.

The Training Union program has been assigned indispensable church tasks. If the Training Union program is to fulfil its role in any church, church leaders must give it support commensurate with its vital work for that church.

For Training Union to survive in any church, church leaders must see it as serious religious education. They must see it as the difference between a full [vital] Christian and a mediocre Christian, between a dynamic and a decadent church. They must see it as discipline for securing a deeper, more intelligent commitment from people. They must see it as the answer to the call for a militant church.[6]

I. THE TASKS OF THE TRAINING UNION PROGRAM

The Training Union program is a unique church program found in no other denomination. The organization conducting it is the second largest in Southern Baptist churches. Training Union has the distinct responsibility for training church members to perform with skill through appropriate involvement in the tasks assigned to it. These tasks are:

Teach systematic theology, Christian ethics, Christian history, and church polity and organization

Give orientation to new church members

Train all church members to worship, witness, learn, and minister daily

Train leaders for the church and the denomination: (1) Discover, recruit, and train potential leaders. (2) Provide for specialized training.

Provide organization and leadership for special projects of the church

---

[6] Albert McClellan, "Training Union Facing a New Day as Servant of the Churches," *The Baptist Training Union Magazine,* Jan., 1965, p. 56. Used by permission.

Provide and interpret information regarding the work of the church and the denomination

1. *Teach Systematic Theology, Christian Ethics, Christian History, and Church Polity and Organization*

This task is discussed in chapter 3. Implementation is accomplished primarily through the content areas of study which are presented in chapter 3. The implications of how the church provides needed training for adult members through the other tasks are discussed briefly in this chapter. (A more comprehensive description is included in *A Church Organized and Functioning* by Howse and Thomason and *The Training Program of a Church*, by Harris.)

2. *Give Orientation to New Church Members*

One of the basic tasks of a church is the proper orientation of new converts and transfer members. This task has not been adequately accomplished in past years, as is evidenced by the large number of church members who are lost annually from active service. Someone has estimated that this number surpasses losses in all of America's armed forces during all of the wars of this century. This tragic situation is one of our most embarrassing indictments. Perhaps, in a rightful zeal to win new converts, the continuation of evangelism through conserving its results has been neglected. As a major step toward correcting this situation, orientation of new church members has been assigned to the Training Union.

The Training Union Department of the Baptist Sunday School Board has led in developing a program of new church member orientation. The purpose of this program is to provide a church with the means of ministering to all new members, while at the same time maintaining the purity and strength of its own fellowship.

The program of new church member orientation in general consists of (1) helping to interpret to the church and to new members the covenant relationship which should exist; (2) counseling concerning the meaning of the salvation experience and the meaning of church membership; (3) graded class instruction in basic areas required for approaching Christian growth and church membership training; and (4) integration into the regular training curriculum of study, fellowship, and service as offered in the unions and departments of the Training Union.

Two sessions of counseling are planned for the first two items listed. These sessions are followed by class instruction. The content of the program of instruction includes three main areas: (1) the source and nature of the new life in Christ; (2) the nature and mission of a church; and (3) the opportunities for growth, service, and witness which the church provides. This program of instruction provides graded resource study books for each age group, Junior through Adult, with a Teacher's Guide for each. The instruction classes are provided with material for ten sessions plus a summary session.

Adequate implementation of this new program should help reject the embarrassingly humorous observations by the late J. B. Gambrell that the Baptists' *grab* in evangelism was greater than their *grip*; and that Baptists were *many*, but not *much*.

Adult department associate directors and union vice-presidents or enlistment leaders are assigned responsibilities for helping the Training Union director of new member orientation in enlisting new adult members in the program. These leaders are responsible also for enlisting the new adult members in their departments and unions for continuing church member training.

3. *Train All Church Members to Worship, Witness, Learn, and Minister Daily*

The functions of a church and, therefore, of church members can be described as worshiping, witnessing, learning, and ministering.

Training to *worship* includes studies in the meaning of worship, forms of worship, and improving worship. Laboratory help should be given to church members for improving their worship as a congregation; as members of other church groups; as families; and in their personal devotions.

Witnessing is not confined to the work of the pastor or other ministers of a church staff. This is a function which should be practiced by every church member. Perhaps the greatest difficulty is that most church members have not been "trained" *how* to witness effectively. Training in this function includes laboratory sessions on learning to develop skills in witnessing effectively. The high ratio of church members to each baptism points out one of the chief problems in Baptist work. Training church members to witness effectively is basic to correcting this problem and to fulfilling the commission of Christ.

Training to perform the function of *learning* is more than merely understanding the basic purposes of the organizations of a church. It is seeing the ministry of Christian education as more than tasks of these organizations—it is seeing them as the church functioning as a fellowship for learning. Teaching, training, music, and missions are not separate arms of a church—they are all the church in a continuing, learning ministry with its members.

To minister is a function of the congregation—not of the pastor alone. This is the whole area of Christian life where one learns to practice love for fellow Christians and others. It is the "cup of water in my [Jesus'] name" concept. (See Mark 9:41.) This function also includes in-service training in visiting the sick, the sorrowing, and those facing times of crisis (such as family difficulties, financial breakdown, moral fractures, emotional problems, and perhaps even difficulties with the law).

Showing Christian empathy and an attitude of helpfulness —even skill in helping—is an action for church members to perform for one another. There are always crises and continuing needs even after the ordained ministers of a church fulfil their responsibilities in this area. Those in need want the assurance of the concern and forgiveness of their peer group—those with whom they work and associate in the community and in the church.

Exercise of this function provides the best antidote to problems which can develop as churches become larger, programs become more crowded, and individuals are accorded less time by their pastors and church staffs.

4. *Train Leaders for the Church and the Denomination:* (1) *Discover, Recruit and Train Potential Leaders.* (2) *Provide for Specialized Training.*

One of the great common denominators of Baptist churches is the continuing need for trained leaders for the church's programs. The needs are acute; they represent one of the major hindrances to churches in accomplishing the mission of Christ. The task of training leaders for the church and the denomination should be assigned to the Training Union.

Discovering potential leaders involves examination of church and organization rolls and talent surveys of the membership. It may include designation of workers with older young people and adults to serve as talent "spotters." Adult department directors and union leaders or presidents are given this special responsibility. They attempt to spot members who seem to have potential leadership talent and give them opportunities to prove and use this ability in the department and union. Names are forwarded to the Training Union director of training. Evaluation by a representative committee or existing administrative group, such as the Training Union council, should follow.

Potential leaders, who have been discovered and recognized as having such qualifications, should be recruited for training. Potential leaders should be approached personally and enlisted for training. The director of training should work with representatives from each of the concerned organizations in the church to give leadership in this effort.

The work of training potential leaders incorporates a comprehensive and balanced curriculum which includes instruction, observation, and internship. Some of the areas covered by this curriculum are: (1) the concept of a church, (2) leadership qualities and techniques, (3) leadership needs within the church, (4) Old and New Testament survey studies, (5) Baptist doctrines and history, and (6) educational techniques and materials.

Observation and analysis should also be included in this program of training. Seeing the right and wrong ways to "lead" and discuss these methods with an experienced trainer will be most profitable.

None of the other training opportunities will be more valuable than the planned period of internship. During this period, the potential leader will be given laboratory experience in exercising leadership.

When a potential leader has completed the program of training, and when he has chosen his specific area of preferred service, he should then be enlisted for specialized training for service in his chosen organization. It is from this reservoir, then, that leaders for the programs of a church will be selected and enlisted when needed.

Special materials outlining planned approaches for accomplishing this task have been prepared to cover a period of approximately twenty-six weeks. They are available in your Baptist Book Store.

5. *Provide Organization and Leadership for Special Projects of the Church*

A church has two alternatives when faced with planning any of a myriad of special projects. It can inaugurate a series of special committees or establish another organization to plan and direct the project; or, it can choose to use an existing organization in the church which is already functioning. The latter choice has more to recommend it. A church should have the organization it needs to accomplish tasks, but it should have no more organization than is actually needed.

The very nature of the work of certain program organizations gives them certain logical responsibilities. A church will likely choose to assign special projects to organizations where such relationship can be seen. When we say that a church assigns responsibility to an organization, we are truly saying that the church is assigning responsibility to itself—

since all organizations are members of the same body, and their officers are officers of the church.

Training Union has had the assignment for certain special projects for many years. Perennial efforts of this organization to train church members to witness include the Church Study Course and Training Union resource units. Through these studies, church members are better prepared for revival efforts and for witnessing in general.

Youth Week is another special training project which Training Union has developed and promoted annually. It inspires adults who, in turn, give encouragement to the youth filling the positions of church leadership for a week.

Church Membership Training Week is an annual project in most churches. Hundreds of thousands of Baptists have engaged in much of their textbook study work during one of these weeks. This project is familiarly known as the "Spring Study Course." It covers many subjects, centering each year on one which is of current priority to Southern Baptists. The Training Union Department of the Baptist Sunday School Board prepares the books and promotional materials for use in the churches.

Training Union has developed and continues to provide leadership for Christian Home Week, Student Night at Christmas, and Watch Night services.

A newer project promoted by Training Union is a clinic, usually in the association, to train church officers and committees. Training Unions, more and more, are being asked to plan and lead such projects in their churches.

Adults in Training Union lead in supporting all of these church projects which are sponsored by the church's training program. They also actively support projects assigned to other program organizations: such as January Bible Study Week (Sunday School); Laymen's Day (Brotherhood); weeks of prayer and mission study weeks (Woman's Missionary Union); and Music Expansion Week (Music Ministry). As other short-term tasks or projects are to be assigned, the church program organization best equipped to provide organization and leadership will be given that responsibility by a church. Adults in Training Union enthusiastically participate in projects which offer opportunities for Christian growth, service, and skill development.

6. Provide and Interpret Information Regarding the Work of the Church and the Denomination

Southern Baptist leaders are frequently approached by leaders of other denominational groups with the question, How do you get such phenomenal cooperation from so many churches? These leaders of other denominations are even more amazed upon learning that Southern Baptists' planning leaders have no authority; that they depend only upon voluntary cooperation to enlist such participation. The true genius of this miracle of spiritual effectiveness can be suggested as being an *informed constituency*. Every member of every Southern Baptist church can know the details of purpose and materials of every suggested endeavor.

Each of the church program organizations has the assigned task of helping inform its members concerning the work of their church and their denomination. The task is divided into two parts: information regarding the work of a church, and information regarding the work of the denomination.

Every "inside" church project should have information disseminated concerning purposes and plans if intelligent cooperative participation is to be secured. This task involves telling the people, telling the people, and telling the people again and again. Church organizations have opportunities through scheduled meetings and planning sessions to accomplish this "telling" job.

Providing information regarding the denomination includes the work of and training opportunities in the association, the first unit in the denomination. It also includes the state convention, the Southern Baptist Convention, and the Baptist World Alliance. Church members need to know why and how their churches link hands voluntarily with other churches in cooperation throughout the community and around the world to accomplish certain purposes. They need to know about the work, purposes, and needs of institutions and agencies of their denomination.

Training Union leaders will not fail to promote the work within their churches and to lift the eyes of their members to see needs and opportunities in a larger fellowship.

This task for Training Union, and the other church program organizations, will become increasingly more operative as the concept of channeling is fully realized. In this relationship, church program organizations "channel" information and help which other programs and services of Southern Baptist agencies wish to communicate to church members.

II. RELATING TRAINING TO ADULT CHURCH MEMBERS

Consideration has been given already to *church* and to *training*. In this section, consideration of the *adult* will be related to the first two elements of the book's title.

1. *Concept of Adulthood*

An attempt to define an adult should be made before investigating his training needs as a church member and before showing what is being done to meet these needs. A superior attempt at a complete definition was developed in the concluding chapter of Luella Cole's *The Psychology of Adolescence* and then summarized in this paragraph:

A true adult is, then, a person of adequate physical and mental development, controlled emotional reactions, and tolerant attitudes; he has the ability to treat others objectively; he is independent of parental control, reasonably satisfied with his point of view toward life, and reasonably happy in his job; he is economically independent; he is not dominated by the opinions of those about him, nor is he in revolt against social conventions; he can get along in ordinary social situations without attracting unfavorable attention; and, above all, he has learned to accept the truth about himself and to face reality instead of either running away from it or making believe it is not there.[7]

[7] Luella Cole, *The Psychology of Adolescence* (New York: Holt, Rinehart and Winston, Inc., 1956), p. 676. Used by permission.

If this definition seems rather long and challenging, let the adult reader attempt to state a shorter one which is adequate. Mrs. Cole's paragraph is at least more palatable than a shorter effort offered by some nameless (with obvious reason) teacher who defined an adult as one who was able to make his out-go equal his in-come!

Many difficulties have developed in considering adults because of a misunderstanding of the word "adult." The word is derived from the Latin verb *adolesco,* meaning to grow.

An adult is neither "grown" nor fully mature at age twenty-one or at age twenty-five. The adult should continue to grow during the rest of his life even as he has in the years preceding what we rather arbitrarily describe as *adulthood.* Modern understanding of the adult is that he is a growing person. This is the essential element in a consideration of this age group. Writers in the field of understanding and working with adults now recognize universally the principle of continuing development.

Malcolm S. Knowles, writing from successful experience and long study and service, began the first chapter of his book *Informal Adult Education* by stating:

Adulthood is a problem. It is also a largely unfulfilled opportunity. It is a problem because our culture makes an assumption about adults that is not true. This is the assumption that adults, because they are adults, are mature. It is the assumption that by the time people reach twenty-one they have learned all they need to know for effective adult living.

Not all adults are mature and probably every adult is immature in some respects.[8]

Mr. Knowles has focused on the term "maturity," which is a key word used by most writers and educators in discussing adulthood. Perhaps Harry A. Overstreet in *The Mature Mind* has best summarized this idea of maturity in what he terms the "maturity concept." He explained the maturity

---

[8] Malcolm S. Knowles, *Informal Adult Education* (New York: Association Press, 1951), p. 3. Used by permission.

concept as the outgrowth of the major psychological and psychiatric discoveries of this era. According to Overstreet, an adult is to mature psychologically as well as physically, to mature along the line of what is unique in him and what he healthily shares with all his fellows, and to continue the maturing process throughout his life. This is the maturity concept.

The concept of an adult as a growing, maturing person, capable of and responsible for continuing to learn is relatively new. Too recently, there was continued popular acceptance of the ill-considered proverb, "You can't teach an old dog new tricks." The implication is that when a person has grown up, he has passed the time of learning. Even William James, a psychologist of recognized authority, once said, "Outside of their own business, the ideas gained by men before they are twenty-five are practically the only ideas they shall have in their lives. They cannot get anything new." [9]

In 1928, the long-established assumption that only childhood is the time for learning was refuted. Educators began to give considerable attention to finding ways to help adults continue to learn better. This was due primarily to the publication of the research and findings of E. L. Thorndike and his associates at Columbia University. Much psychological data and many varieties of specifically devised experiments with adult groups have continued to show that adults have the ability to continue to learn.

It has been established that adults possess the same capacity for knowledge, skills, and appreciations at 40, 50, and even 60 years of age as they had at age 20. Learning tasks which place a premium on speed become a bit more difficult after middle age, but this indicates only a slowing of the rate of learning, not of the ability to learn. This declining rate is very gradual and continues generally as long as a person lives. Leaders of educational programs need to rec-

---

[9] William James, *The Principles of Psychology*, Vol. II, p. 402, cited by Edward L. Thorndike, et al., *Adult Learning* (New York: The Macmillan Co., 1928), p. 3.

ognize more the increase in learning ability which adults bring to the learning situation—that which is contributed by experience, helping to make relevant and applicable the learning. This priceless ingredient is not possessed by youth.

As psychologists and educators have carried further what Thorndike began, it has become increasingly apparent that human beings can and must—for their own sakes and that of a changing world—learn new facts and insights as long as they live. This is especially true in the learning fellowship of a church.

When planning church training programs, it is not only important to recognize the concept that the adult is a growing person capable of learning; it is also vitally essential to recognize that not all adults are alike. Adulthood should be divided into at least four distinct periods: *early, middle, late middle,* and *senior.* There are more changes, physically and psychologically, occurring in the adult years than perhaps any other period except birth through puberty. Each of the periods of adulthood has distinct characteristics which are considered by curriculum planners. There are physical, mental, social, and spiritual characteristics peculiar to each period. These do effect changes in the needs of adults and in the most effective learning procedures for meeting these needs.

2. *The Adult as a Church Recruit*

Although a study of adulthood generally is a fascinating subject for all who would work in a program of training for this age group, the real job of relating the training ministry of a church to its adult members can best be seen by considering specifically the needs of *an* adult. The following case study does not describe the most typical experiences of adult members in our churches today. However, it can be the testimony of millions of adults whom we are now challenged to reach for Christ. This case study offers a perspective of several church programs functioning together.

Consider a man approximately 35 to 40 years of age who is married and has two children. Consider that he has just moved into a home in a neighborhood within the ministering area of your church. Create a picture now—a moving picture of typical events in his becoming a part of your church—enlisting in a mighty army which is to do battle against the forces of evil in this world.

(1) *Reached by the Sunday School.*—Hearing of the family's presence in the community, members of church organizations go to visit the various members of the family who are prospects for their classes, unions, choirs, circles, chapters, or other units. These members go representing the church. The warmth of their personal interest and their offers of practical help result in the new family's agreeing to be taken to the services on the next Sunday as guests of a church family.

On Sunday morning, members of the prospect family are scattered over the church buildings in graded classes, studying the biblical revelation. The husband and father is not a Christian and has had neither background nor experience in a Christian home or church. He has presented to him by a wise teacher (within the context of any lesson scheduled for study) what the Bible reveals concerning redemption. In the Sunday School capable teachers who are concerned with the primary task of reaching the unsaved, can always include in a lesson presentation appropriate Scripture references concerning what the Bible reveals about man's lost condition and how he may be saved. This may be the first knowledge on this subject ever gained by this prospect.

(2) *Committed in the worship service.*—Later, in the worship service, the unsaved prospect and his family are surrounded by an atmosphere of warmth and reverent fellowship. They are impressed by the smiles of greeting and handclasps of friendship. An impact is made upon them by the congregation's hearty participation in singing, in praying, in the giving of offerings, in the special music, and in their reading of the Bible.

Then the service focuses upon the pulpit and proclamation as God's messenger stands in his place to interpret and exhort from God's Word. As the pastor preaches, the prospect finds that the message applies to his own condition. With the presence of the Holy Spirit, the unsaved man's conscience is pricked. He notes passages which describe him and which describe spiritual responses which he begins to consider as personal actions.

During the invitation, as the congregation sings and prays, the Holy Spirit works in convicting application of the message until the lost father says in his heart, *These promises of God fill needs which I recognize in my life*. He walks the aisle, and gives his hand to the pastor as a token of acceptance of Christ for salvation.

This act does not end the work of evangelism. In the next few minutes this man stands before the congregation and says some things to them. The congregation responds by saying some things to him. Hearing these voices with spiritual ears can form the basis of correcting the inadequate reception and assimilation of new converts into the fellowship of many Baptist churches.

A recording of what the new convert is saying in his heart, if not vocally heard, would probably read:

I have a great joy in my heart. This joy is there because Jesus has saved my soul. However, this joy creates in me an urgent desire to serve Jesus—to express in service my response for what he has done for me. This gives me a strong hunger, because I do not know *how* to serve him. I know nothing about the Christian life—how a Christian should walk and talk and conduct himself before his family, in society, and in his business. I know nothing of the stand a Christian should take on moral and civic issues. I do not know how to use my Bible. I do not know how to serve.

As the new convert looks at the congregation, he continues:

You know how to serve Jesus. You have been Christians for many years. Many of you have taught the Bible. You have raised Christian families and have established yourselves as Christians in the eyes of this community. So, I am asking that you let me become a part of this fellowship in this church; that you help me learn the things I need to learn and do the things I need to do if I am going to be able to do something for Jesus.

And as the members of that church face the new convert, they say to him, both individually and collectively, as surely as they authorize his baptism:

We pledge to you, our new Christian brother, that we will do all that we can to help you learn the things you need to learn, and to do the things you need to do to be a witness and servant for Christ through his church.

(3) *Trained in the Training Union.*—Just as a new recruit in the army needs training before going to battle, so the new volunteer in the Christian army needs training. A tragedy occurs when members of the military are involved in battle before having had sufficient training. This was illustrated vividly during the latter days of conflict in the European theater during World War II. When the German army made an unexpected breakthrough in the Ardennes forests of Belgium, casualties were high for the American forces. Replacements had to be sent into the lines rapidly. A tragic, futile feeling came to observers each day as they watched many of these replacements, who had just come into combat units on the previous night, being carried out as casualties by morning—many with their uniforms undirtied and their weapons unfired. The reason? They had been insufficiently trained. They had been rushed from recruit training into battle. The replacements were casualties because they did not really know what was going on. They were not able to make a contribution to the effort of their units; they were not even able to care for themselves.

This same tragically futile feeling comes when we see tender new converts thrown into the spiritual warfare which abounds on every front. Many of these casualties from active participation and service can be avoided if adequate training is administered by a concerned church fellowship. This is the mission of Training Union for the adult in this case study. In the training agency of this church the new convert will receive training to equip him as a lasting, effective warrior for Christ.

The need for training never ceases. Military personnel must continue training as long as they are eligible for duty.

Professional athletes, accomplished musicians, doctors, businessmen, farmers, teachers, pilots, and plumbers have to continue training in order to maintain skills and to employ the latest materials and best techniques.

Satan never slackens his efforts to weaken and capture the Christian soldier. Paul wrote to the young preacher Timothy: "Keep yourself in training for the practice of religion" (1 Tim. 4:7, NEB*). In Christ's army, members of a church must continue their training activity throughout life.

3. What a Church Promises the Adult Member

When the new member is received by a church, he and the congregation enter into a covenant relationship. This relationship truly constitutes what we define as church membership, and it begins with the church's requirements for membership. Being a Christian is not the only requirement for membership in a church. When a new member enters into the covenant relationship with his church, it means that he accepts the doctrines, discipline, and goals of that church. The question which is really being asked by that congregation is, Are you a Christian who can come into our fellowship, who can share happily in our doctrines, in our discipline, and in our goals, and so find in us resources needed to fulfil the call which you now have from Christ?

(1) Responsibilities Inherent in the Covenant Relationship

Many responsibilities are assumed by a church and pledged to its members. A church offers to administer baptism (Acts 2:41; Rom. 6:1–4); pledges to love this new brother even though he fall (Matt. 18:21–35); and to provide opportunities for growth and involvement in the Christian life. A church assumes a responsibility to provide a fellowship of regenerate church members as a family of God (John 3:3; Acts 4:4). A church will minister in times of crises (Phil. 4:3; 1 Thess. 5:15–18) and share in a service

---

* The New English Bible © The Delegates of the University Press and the Syndics of the Cambridge University Press, 1961. Used by permission.

fellowship which reaches around the world in its witness for Christ (Acts 13:2).

A church also should assume some specific responsibilities in the area of training new converts and all members.

(2) *Types of Training.*—Not all training will be of the same type. Different types of training are:

—*New Church Member Orientation* (approximately 13 sessions in counseling and graded classwork)

—*Church Member Training* (on a continuing basis for all church members)

—*Potential Leader Training* (approximately 26 sessions initially, with additional sessions as needed)

—*Specialized Leader Training* (sessions as needed)

The illustration on page 36 shows the types of training. The base represents initial training for new members. The stacking rod represents the continuing training in which all church members engage. The two rings are symbols of the other types of training in which some members will participate. These rings can be added around the continuing church member training, in which every member continues to train even when potential leader training and specialized leader training are completed, unless they are leading these groups.

These are the types of training provided for church members and leaders. The new recruit, won through the outreach of the Sunday School, the impact of worship, and the faithful proclamation of a church, is inducted into the army of the church through new church member orientation.

After his orientation through counseling and classwork, the new member begins his church member training. This training is "on the front lines," as it were, since he will be engaged in "doing" as a part of his training. He participates in training sessions in systematic theology, Christian ethics, Christian history, and church polity and organization. In the front lines of Christian warfare, he is to train in worshiping, witnessing, learning, and ministering daily. He develops skills in group action which will help his church to achieve its purposes in the world.

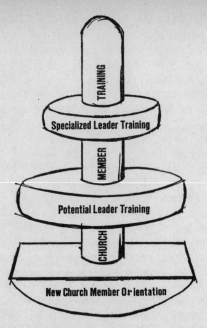

In addition to church member training, Training Union provides church leader training. This includes potential leader training and specialized leader training. If a member has the potential for serving as a leader in his church, this potential should be discovered. He can be recruited to commit himself to potential leader training to develop these leadership capacities. In this type of training, he engages in comprehensive class study, observation, laboratory work, and a period of internship.

An additional step, which the church should offer qualified members as needed, is specialized leader training. This responsibility of providing training for specialized leaders is carried by the church program organizations with the assistance of the Training Union. All five organizations are responsible for training their own leaders. The Training Union serves the other church program organizations by developing a comprehensive plan for leader training, arranging training schedules, and assisting in the enlistment of leaders for the training activities. The Training Union does not seek to provide the content for the other four organizations in this type of training. Each program develops its own content, the use of which helps this member to become skilful as a church leader in his particular area.

4. *What an Adult Member Promises His Church*

In the covenant relationship established between the new church member and his church, the candidate for membership promises to assume certain responsibilities.

(1) *To honor and sustain his church.*—This conveys that he will try to be regular in his attendance.

(2) *To love and help fellow church members.*—This may be expressed in such ways as intercessory prayer, aid in times of need, and sympathy and courtesy.

(3) *To live a consistent Christian life.*—This involves any changes in social or business and family relations which may be necessary.

(4) *To grow as a maturing Christian.*—This suggests using opportunities for study and training as natural and necessary for spiritual growth.

(5) *To serve in and through his church.*—This implies accepting responsibility for performing tasks commensurate with his abilities and the needs of the church.

The picture of a new Christian and church member has been presented. He has come into the fellowship of a church and has many needs. The new member has asked that he be taught and trained to fill the needs which will make him capable of service. Gradually, he has learned facts and concepts, and has had opportunity to develop the facility for expressing himself on spiritual matters in small, like-minded, encouraging groups of fellow believers. He has then found himself better able to give expression concerning his Christian convictions in other groups which are not so conducive to Christian expression, perhaps even antagonistic. The new member is able to perform as a witness. He will begin to bear the true fruit of a Christian. This is the God-given ambition that was put in his heart during the moments when he stood in the first, full, fresh glow of the salvation experience. Through training, his church has helped him to accomplish this goal. He will accomplish it again and again in the divine pattern established by Christ Jesus for winning the world to his kingdom.

SUMMARY

A church, by its nature and functions, has tasks which demand the training of Adult members if it is to be a strong church in doing the work of Christ. Adult members, by their natures, have the capacity to grow. By the covenant they have made with their churches, they desire to be trained to serve Christ. Churches have provided a training program which is offered to Adults. As Adults grow in the training program, they will be able to accomplish the Spirit-given goal of serving their Lord through their churches.

CHAPTER 3

I. TRAINING UNION'S METHOD FOR ACCOMPLISHING ITS CURRICU-
   LUM
II. COURSES OF STUDY
   1. Lesson Courses
   2. Church Study Course
   3. Bible Readers' Course

3

Content for Training Adults
Is Provided

WE COME NOW to an assessment of the content which is provided to help a church in its program for training adults. Another way of stating it in educational terms is to say that we now approach, in the next several chapters, a discussion of how a church can "accomplish its curriculum" for training adult church members.

The term "accomplishing" as used here may be understood after the word "curriculum" has been adequately defined. "Curriculum" was used by the ancient Romans to describe the running which a man does in a race, suggesting a goal and the activity which takes a runner to that goal. Educators found this word to be appropriate to describe their work. They also had goals, and their task was to guide pupils in activities which would lead them over the course to the destination. The writer of Hebrews described curriculum when he urged the readers of his epistle to "run with patience the race" (Heb. 12:1) which was set before them. He then proceeded for two chapters to describe activities which were to be a part of the course of that race which would take the Christian toward the goal of being made "perfect in every good work to do his will" (Heb. 13:21).

In this generation there have been numerous writers in the field of religious education who have explicitly described the meaning of the term "curriculum" in its full sense. W. L. Howse has described an adequate concept of curriculum as recognizing more than the subject matter:

The curriculum is all those activities . . . participated in by the pupil . . . which will bring about results in the life and conduct of the pupil. Broadly stated, the curriculum will include worship, service, study, social and recreational activities, and experiences in religion.[1]

Perhaps the most succinct reference to curriculum—one which encompasses most of what has been cited from other writers—is given by Harper in this statement: "The modern curriculum of religious education should consist of materials, methods, and organization." [2]

I. TRAINING UNION'S METHOD FOR ACCOMPLISHING ITS CURRICULUM

Method is the way in which a thing is accomplished. It is the manner or procedure used in getting the desired results. Method has been described as "The bringing about of conditions under which experience may be enriched, modified, controlled, understood, and redirected in terms of responsible participation." [3]

The educational method used in a church's training program for adults is unique. It must be unique, for there is an unusual learning situation to be met. In the customary learning setting, three elements are considered necessary. These are (1) the learners, (2) that which is to be learned, and (3) a teacher. The teacher is to interpret that which is to be learned to the learners, guiding their learning experiences. In the Training Union Program for adults, however, one of these three elements has been removed. There are learners and there is a content to be learned, but there is no one designated as teacher. Something must come into the learning situation to assume at least a portion of the role of the teacher if the learners are to be able to interpret the materials of instruction.

---

[1] William Lewis Howse, "The Education Director" (Unpublished D.R.E. thesis, Department of Administration, School of Religious Education, Southwestern Baptist Theological Seminary, 1937), p. 167.

[2] W. A. Harper, *The Minister of Education* (Ashland, Ohio: The University Post Publishing Company, 1939), p. 33.

[3] *Ibid.*, p. 131.

An officer or designated group member leads in planning and stimulates the learners in their own learning experiences. Key expressions in this approach are "group learning" and "individual participation." All educational techniques may be used, including the lecture, for imparting a body of content or instructing in a skill. However, the union members will have participated as a group in planning, discussing, and applying this learning experience.

The method of individual participation is utilized in all three of the elements which comprise the method or strategy of Training Union in accomplishing its curriculum with adults. These elements, which really constitute the curriculum will be discussed as: (1) *courses of study*; (2) *organization*; and (3) *activities* (which include those of planning, meeting, and evaluating).

II. COURSES OF STUDY

An adequate concept of curriculum has been shown to include more than the content of the courses studied. However, participation in these courses is used to instill the needed items of church membership training into the life of the person being trained. In Training Union there are three courses of study for adults: (1) *lesson courses*; (2) *Church Study Course*; and (3) *Bible Readers' Course*.

1. *Lesson Courses*

(1) *Relation to content areas.*—The term "lesson courses" is used to describe the materials designed for study and discussion by the members in the weekly meetings. These sessions are planned by units, each unit relating to one (or more) areas of study. An area of study is "any basic area of content which requires continuing study on the part of the congregation if the church is to achieve its objectives." [4]

These content areas have been delineated from the statement of tasks assigned to the Training Union by a church.

---

[4] W. L. Howse and W. O. Thomason, *A Church Organized and Functioning* (Nashville: Convention Press, 1963), p. 13.

Basic subjects as named in the Training Union content areas are (1) systematic theology, (2) Christian ethics, (3) Christian history, (4) church polity and organization.

Each year, units of study in each of the content areas are offered in the lesson courses for Adults. Obviously, not every subject which can be classified under each content area will be given attention annually. It is necessary, therefore, to treat some subjects in subsequent years. Therefore, church members must participate over a period of years to get a basic understanding of these areas and the "refresher studies" in them.

The basic reason for every church member participating in Training Union is to experience a fellowship of study and training with these areas providing basic content. Every church member should have continuing learning experiences. He should take into his life the elements of these basic content areas which will contribute to the development of needed skills for Christian action in and through the church.

(2) *Description and relevance of content areas.*—To understand the importance of the content areas, consider the following statement or definition of each.

Systematic Theology.—Theology is a study of the truths about God and his relationship to man. Systematic theology attempts to organize these truths into a logical, orderly system of Christian doctrine.

Baptist church members who have had a reasonable opportunity to study in the educational organizations of their churches probably know a great deal more about what they believe than they realize. The difficulty often comes because they have not systematized or organized their beliefs into logical statements which they can share readily when asked what they believe. When representatives of other faiths or sects ask a series of probing questions, Baptists many times become embarrassed by not having a ready answer. They then confuse embarrassment with lack of knowledge. From lack of knowledge doubt arises, and sometimes this doubt turns to unbelief. These church members are prime victims then for man-made doctrines which are arranged in logical, quick-for-humans-to-grasp patterns.

Baptists need to learn to systematize their beliefs so that they can readily fulfil the admonition given in 1 Peter 3:15: "But sanctify the Lord God in your hearts: and be ready always to give an answer to every man that asketh you a reason of the hope that is in you with meekness and fear."

Christian Ethics.—Ethics has been defined as the "ought-ness" of the Christian experience in its practical application. Ethics is rooted in theology and receives its imperative for application from what God has done for man in and through Jesus Christ.

The field of Christian ethics includes such critical areas for the Christian as language, Lord's Day observance, honesty, family life, vocations, alcohol education, moral conduct, social practices, Christian citizenship, labor and management relations, race relations, and other equally important subjects of continuing interest to all church members.

Christian History.—Christian history is the story of the origin and development of Christianity and of its influence upon the world.

Baptists have perhaps the richest history of any denomination. The lack of knowledge in this area on the part of Baptists is a tragedy. We must study history's description of events. In the current arena of world need and spiritual warfare we must use the lessons learned and action patterns proved by our Christian forebears.

A study of Christian history includes a study of New Testament churches, as well as a study of the background for Christianity revealed in the Old Testament. This area of study traces the development of Christianity, including the history of Christian missions, down through the centuries. Attention is given to Baptist groups, especially Southern Baptists.

Church Polity and Organization.—Church polity and organization refers to how a church governs itself and organizes to fulfil its mission.

A Baptist church is unlike any other organization or institution. It is primarily a fellowship. Baptist churches, however, look to the New Testament as their rule of faith and practice. Baptists have developed a form of church government which, though unique and sometimes not easily understood, works very well for our particular practice of churchmanship.

Some Baptist church members who have backgrounds of other faiths often find it difficult to understand the practices which Baptists use to govern themselves. Frequently, disharmony develops when these members try to bring over into the framework of a Baptist church practices which seem to work well in other kinds of churches. This is also true when members try to bring into a Baptist church a system for "running the church" which is successful in business or government. Many problems in the fellowship will be avoided when members have adequate opportunities to study Baptist church polity and organization.

(3) *Materials to implement content areas.*—Adults in Training Union are provided with two curriculums which include two basic quarterlies each. The two curriculums are the Life and Work Curriculum and the Christian Training Curriculum. (The Christian Training Curriculum also includes two special quarterlies.) The purposes of the two curriculums and descriptions of the quarterlies follow:

Life and Work Curriculum.—Beginning in the fall quarter of 1966, the Life and Work Curriculum provides a new curriculum for Adults and Young People. It can be used in churches of all sizes.

There are three basic principles on which the Life and Work Curriculum is built. This curriculum is (1) *Bible-based,* (2) *church-oriented,* and (3) *action-inducing.* It is designed to provide *Bible* study which leads the learners to understand better the life and work of a *church.* The increased understanding of the nature and functions of a church as revealed in the Bible should result in more appropriate *action* by members of a church.

In the Life and Work Curriculum, the curriculum materials of the Sunday School, Training Union, Brotherhood,

Woman's Missionary Union, and Music Ministry are *corre-lated*. The suggested actions which logically grow out of this guided Bible study are *coordinated* to help a church achieve its goals. The purpose of this curriculum then is to provide the unified support of each of the church program organizations to the total work of a church.

The Life and Work Curriculum focuses on the concept that Scriptures concerning the life and work of New Testament churches form an important part of the content for implementing the church function of learning. Special attention is given to biblical studies concerning the nature, purpose, functions, and tasks of a church. Learners in the organizations are encouraged to *act* on what they learn. Appropriate, coordinated *actions* are suggested in the curriculum materials for each of the church program organizations.

The Sunday School lessons of the Life and Work Curriculum are prepared first. Then Training Union, Woman's Missionary Union, Brotherhood, and Music Ministry materials, are written to correlate with the Sunday School materials and with one another. The Church Administration Department works with the curriculum planners of these five church program organizations to plan coordinated suggested church actions which will logically grow out of these studies.

The Training Union Life and Work Curriculum provides two basic quarterlies for use in Adult unions. *Adults Training for Action, A Personal Training Guide* is used by each member for study preparation. It is designed also for use by Adults who cannot or do not attend group sessions. The *Adult Training Guide, A Group Training Guide* is used by study leaders, group captains, and others who are responsible for planning, conducting, and evaluating activities based on the lesson courses. See chapter 6 for a discussion of the planning and the leaders who are to accomplish it.

Adults Training for Action, A Personal Training Guide includes thirteen articles (or training session reading resource material), one for each week in the quarter. The section for the Bible Readers' Course includes daily reading references, themes, devotional comments, and the missionary prayer calendar. Other appropriate items will be included each quarter. These will be in the nature of interest-builders, provocative ideas, tests for preview and review on content, puzzles, and other exercises, such as analyzing graphs, interpreting tables, and the like.

In the *Adult Training Guide, A Group Training Guide,* officers involved in planning training sessions will find a section with specific suggestions for planning and conducting each session of the units provided for use that quarter. "Training Procedures" offers methods, resources, learning aids, Scripture references, and so on. Suggested ways of correlating these studies with those of the other church program organizations are given. "Advanced Training Procedures" suggests similar activities and resources requiring more advanced work. These procedures are designed for unions which are willing to do advanced work. "Special Training Procedures" will appear when the study of a particular subject demands a distinct consideration of the materials for special groups, such as single adults, senior adults, and others.

Each *Group Training Guide* includes an undated unit. This unit usually consists of a bibliography, suggested outlines, and training procedures. Its basic purpose is to provide for unions an opportunity to select units which best meet their needs. Generally, it is directed to the study leader or group captain and uses outside resource materials.

Each *Group Training Guide* also contains special learning aids. For example, a brief flip chart might be inserted as pages in the center of the periodical. Separate curriculum supplements and learning aids will be provided when appropriate to the content studies.

Christian Training Curriculum.—The Christian Training Curriculum for Adults is correlated, where possible, with the Uniform Sunday School lesson course. It provides two basic quarterlies.

The first, *Baptist Adults, A Personal Training Guide,* provides thirteen study articles each quarter. This periodical is similar to the former *Baptist Adults.* It is somewhat more traditional in approach and format. However, this quarterly contains many of the same features as *Adults Training for Action, A Personal Training Guide* described in the Life and Work Curriculum.

Training Adults, A Group Training Guide should be provided for officers concerned with planning, conducting, and evaluating training sessions based on the lesson courses in the Christian Training Curriculum. The features for this quarterly are similar to the *Adult Training Guide, A Group Training Guide* described in the Life and Work Curriculum. The format and design is similar, but the training procedures, learning aids, resources, and activities relate to the content of the units in the Christian Training Curriculum.

In addition to the two basic quarterlies, two special quarterlies also are provided in the Christian Training Curriculum: *Training Union Quarterly Simplified* and *La Fe Bautista*.

Training Union Quarterly Simplified carries an adaptation of the lesson course material in *Baptist Adults, A Personal Training Guide.* This periodical is prepared for persons with limited educational background; for persons who are beginning to learn English; for new adult readers; and for the deaf. The material is easy to read because of the large print and the simple language. Along with the study material, *Training Union Quarterly Simplified* includes a word list or glossary of difficult terms and a simple training procedure or discussion guide for each training session.

La Fe Bautista (The Baptist Faith) is a Spanish edition of *Training Union Quarterly Simplified.* It is prepared for Spanish-speaking people in the United States. (There is a quarterly for Adult union members in Spanish-speaking countries outside the United States. It is published by the Spanish Baptist Publishing House, El Paso, Texas, an agency of the Foreign Mission Board of the Southern Baptist Convention.) In addition to the study materials, *La Fe Bautista* includes a leadership section of current interest to church leaders. It presents information concerning general church work and the work of the denomination.

ADULT LESSON COURSE MATERIALS

Two Curriculums	Four Basic Quarterlies
1. Life and Work Curriculum (Correlated with Life and Work Curriculum of Sunday School and other organizations)	*Adults Training for Action, A Personal Training Guide* *Adult Training Guide, A Group Training Guide*
2. Christian Training Curriculum (For churches that use Uniform Lesson materials in Sunday School)	*Baptist Adults, A Personal Training Guide* *Training Adults, A Group Training Guide*
	PLUS TWO SPECIAL QUARTERLIES *Training Union Quarterly Simplified* (An adaptation of *Baptist Adults,* with large print and simplified language) *La Fe Bautista* (An edition of *Training Union Quarterly Simplified* for Spanish-speaking people in the United States)

Choosing Between the Two Curriculums.—Each church decides which of the two curriculums to use for its Sunday School and Training Union. (Brotherhood, Woman's Missionary Union, and Music Ministry will provide only the Life and Work Curriculum.) The recommendation as to which curriculum to use will probably be made by the church council. The following facts may be pertinent in considering a choice of Training Union curriculum materials:

Both curriculums are related to the Southern Baptist Convention annual emphases. The Life and Work Curriculum is more closely related.

Both curriculums are usable in a church regardless of the number of program organizations.

Helps for both curriculums are provided in *The Baptist Training Union Magazine*.

Both curriculums are usable with either the regular or alternate organization plan for Adult unions.

The cost of quarterlies is the same for both curriculums.

Training Union Life and Work Curriculum relates closely (in Bible-based subject material and suggested church actions) to Sunday School Life and Work Curriculum materials and to those of Brotherhood, Woman's Missionary Union, and Music Ministry. If a church uses Sunday School Life and Work Curriculum, it should also use the Training Union Life and Work Curriculum.

The Training Union Christian Training Curriculum relates appropriately when possible to the Sunday School Uniform lessons. If the Sunday School uses Uniform Lesson series, the Training Union should choose the Christian Training Curriculum.

Training Union Christian Training Curriculum helps members to feel that their training program has not changed drastically. Materials more nearly resemble previous curriculum items.

Resource Units.—Training Union resource units for Adults are booklets containing material which can be substituted for units in the lesson course quarterlies. A resource unit includes a bibliography of suggested resource materials, preparation checklists for the leader, discussion and planning guides, and selected resource materials for study and use in member assignments by the leader. They are "do-it-yourself" units which rely heavily upon individual initiative and outside resources.

Three or four copies of a resource unit are needed in a union—one each for members of the planning team and one for the study leader or group captain. The available units are listed on the regular church literature order blank for periodicals published by the Baptist Sunday School Board.

Resource units may be used (1) during the regular Training Union hour on Sunday evening; (2) during special soul-winning studies prior to revivals; (3) during backyard study courses; (4) during Christian Home Week or other special weeks of emphasis when the subject material is appropriate; (5) for meeting the needs of special interest groups who may wish to conduct studies at other times; and (6) for potential or specialized leadership training groups.

Training Union Curriculum Supplements.—Curriculum supplements for Training Union lesson courses are listed on the church literature order blank each quarter. They may be ordered along with other church literature. These supplements include such items as flip charts, sentence strip charts, record albums, picture sets, and resource packets.

Curriculum supplements help to accomplish two basic purposes: (1) They make additional audio-visual content material available during the study of a unit. (2) They stimulate leaders in the use of a variety of interesting aids and procedures. Here are some of the values of using curriculum supplements.

Such items provide additional material which cannot be included in the basic Training Union quarterlies.

Supplements provide the visual or audio element which heightens interest and understanding beyond that of printed resource study material.

Large charts enable the study leader to make use of individual or group reading. Both the visual impact and the oral repetition aid learning.

Material presented visually not only serves to aid understanding and retention but also encourages individual responses from members.

The use of audio and visual materials makes possible group participation in listening teams and evaluation groups.

Many curriculum supplements, though planned for use with specific units of study, are also usable along with study course books, future study units in the same subject area, and other study groups concerned with these subjects.

Curriculum supplements are prepared to be filed in the church library (resource center) for future studies.

(4) *Analysis by Tests of Good Curriculum Materials.*—The lesson courses for Adults in Training Union are planned and written to stand the following tests which curriculum

builders and other educators agree are required: comprehensiveness, balance, continuity and sequence, flexibility, and learner-involvement.

Comprehensiveness.—To be comprehensive, good curriculum materials should include study opportunities in all of the areas which relate directly to the goals of the group. This means that each of the four content areas is given attention as it relates to church goals.

Balance.—Good study materials should provide a balance of study opportunities in the various areas which are to be included. Periodically, the lesson courses give some attention to all of the basic areas. They also provide an appropriate balance in terms of current emphases and other factors that affect relevancy.

Churches and unions are given a great deal of selectivity in their choice of materials from the lesson courses. The matter of balance needs to be kept in mind as these groups plan to use the materials from the quarterlies and/or resource units. Curriculum planning teams and editors have exercised care in providing for a balanced plan of study and training in these publications. Usually, when unions or churches inadvisedly go outside these published lesson course materials for study resources, the balance is destroyed.

Continuity and Sequence.—It is important that all areas be given attention and that a balance of emphasis be planned. It is also important to plan the way in which one unit of study may follow another. The time of the year when certain units are related to other church activities and organizational emphases and the ways in which materials correlate with one another must be considered. This sequence, which draws the learner logically from one unit to another in a balanced and comprehensive set of study materials, is built into the basic course of study in a single quarterly. However, with the range of selectivity afforded as church (between curriculums) and a union (between units), attention should be given to this principle when making selections.

Flexibility.—Training Union curriculum is flexible in order to meet the varying needs of individual learners. This
flexibility is important because of the learners' differing backgrounds of interest, spiritual maturity, and academic
training, as well as the varying needs of churches and individual groups within those churches. This flexibility makes
possible adaptation to meet the needs of individual learners,
learning groups, and churches. Flexibility is found in content, depth, and scheduling.

Training Union lesson course material for Adults is flexible
in content. Each issue of the Group Training Guide in the
two curriculums includes an undated unit in addition to
the dated units (13 articles). To help members choose the
studies most appropriate for them, a Unit Selection Plan is
included in each of these quarterlies. Following this plan,
members of each union may choose to study subjects or
units that they feel will best meet their individual needs in
the union and in the church at that particular time.

Training Union lesson course material for Adults is flexible in depth. The variety in depth ranges from simple language for persons of limited formal education to challenging
references for further study for those who wish to deepen
their investigation of a particular subject area. Alternate
training procedures are offered with the suggestion that
study leaders or group captains adapt and use them in ways
appropriate to the members of their unions. There are training procedures appropriate for unions in which members
are unable or unwilling to do little more than "give parts."
Advance training procedures in the same quarterlies provide
more challenging outlines and bibliographies of additional
resources outside the quarterlies.

Training Union lesson course material for Adults is flexible in scheduling. Although most of the units will be used
on Sunday evenings, studies may be conducted at other
times. Unions frequently find that their interests and needs
during a quarter cannot be met in only thirteen weekly
meetings. Weeknight studies are frequently arranged for
working groups. Other unions, comprised mainly of retirees,

find daytime hours profitable for such additional study. For special interests groups, sessions can be arranged during other regular church meetings, such as on Wednesday evenings or Sundays.

In addition to this adaptation which unions may make in scheduling, each Group Training Guide contains an undated unit. Unions may choose to use the undated units at any appropriate time during the year. A sufficient number of all quarterlies should be filed in the church library so that unions may exercise flexibility in scheduling by being assured that resource materials will be available for all units at a later date.

Learner-involvement.—Good Training Union lesson course materials are designed so that learners become actively involved in the learning experiences. Special helps are prepared for study leaders to use in planning the sessions so that they can more logically and effectively induce learners to become involved. These helps implement the "Guides in Planning for Learning." (See chap. 6 for detailed explanation.) These guides include suggestions for (1) relating each session to the continuity of the unit; (2) defining an aim which is designed or accepted by union members; (3) selecting appropriate methods for participation; (4) preparing learning aids; (5) suggesting follow-through application in individual daily lives; (6) evaluating the sessions for their effectiveness in accomplishing stated aims or learning goals.

2. Church Study Course

The Church Study Course is a membership and leadership course of study which provides textbooks for study in twenty categories needed by church members for Christian growth and leadership development.

Over one hundred books for Adults are included in the Church Study Course. These books form excellent study materials for group study, home study, supplementary resource reading for lesson course studies, educational institutions, and devotional reading.

A system of awards, recognizing completion of requirements for depth study of books in the Church Study Course, has been devised with appropriate recognition diplomas and seals. Requirements are listed on page viii of this book. There are five diplomas. The completion of each diploma with its seals requires the study of twenty books—or a total of one hundred books to complete the awards series. Completing the requirements for all these awards is a worthy and challenging goal for adult church members who desire appropriate opportunities for Christian growth and training for enlarged service in and through their churches.

3. *Bible Readers' Course*

The Bible Readers' Course continues to be a strong emphasis in Training Union. Its use along with the Missionary Prayer Calendar has blessed millions of church members since it was first designed for the B.Y.P.U. and later appropriated by other church program organizations.

Training Union and Sunday School now work together in this significant training task. Training Union trains people by helping them to form the daily habit of Bible reading. Sunday School also encourages members to read daily. Both private devotions and family worship are aided by this course of Bible reading and prayer.

The Bible Readers' Course trains individuals in the skill of using their Bibles—in learning to study the Bible, in finding Scripture references, in reading meditatively and aloud, and in developing a facility for using the Bible. Training Union trains members to develop a sensitivity in applying the truths of the Scriptures to current needs.

CHAPTER 4

I. PRINCIPLES OF ORGANIZATION
   1. Definitions of Organization
   2. Organization as a Spiritual Tool
   3. Organization as an Educational Tool

II. SOME ELEMENTS IN ORGANIZATION
   1. Classification by Congenial Groups
   2. The Group as an Instrument in Learning
   3. Organizational Framework

III. REGULAR ADULT UNION ORGANIZATION
   1. An Adult Union Organized
   2. Training Relationships Charted
   3. Election of Officers Described
   4. Responsibilities of Officers and Committees Assigned

4

Organization for Training Adults Is Recommended

THE TRAINING UNION is a church program organization of Southern Baptists which has been assigned tasks to help church members perform as members of the body of Christ.

A Baptist adult union seeks to implement, or accomplish, the church tasks of Training Union for Adult church members. The union does this by using *courses of study, organization, meetings,* and *activities.*

In chapter 3, the courses of study were examined. Organization will be considered. Principles and elements will be discussed, and organizational patterns for adult unions and departments will be presented.

I. PRINCIPLES OF ORGANIZATION

Organization is necessary in life today. It is needed if an individual is to deliver papers properly or plow a field effectively. To see organization in its proper role, we should understand what it is and the principles which call for its application in the spiritual work of a church.

1. *Definitions of Organization*

To organize has been defined as: "to bring into systematic relation as parts of a whole." [1]

The following quotation helps to clarify what organization is and how it is generally used.

It is by means of organization of a suitable kind that fundamental things get done. For organization is imperative in the dis-

[1] *The Desk Standard Dictionary of the English Language* (New York: Funk & Wagnalls Company, 1946), p. 550.

charge of functions. It is found everywhere "in nature," from electrons to galactic systems, and from the ant hill to the drainage systems of continents.[2]

Organization, as properly conceived and practiced in a Baptist church, can be defined as *how church members arrange themselves in the best possible position to be used effectively by the Holy Spirit.*

2. *Organization as a Spiritual Tool*

Organization, as discussed in chapter 1, has spiritual connotations. These are revealed scripturally in the Old Testament as God led the children of Israel, in the work of Jesus, and in the life of New Testament churches. Organization is used for spiritual purposes in the current life and work of a church. A church is seen as both an organism and as an organization. Organization is used to heighten the effectiveness of the worship services, the observance of the ordinances, the discovery of and witness to the lost, and the church programs of education.

In a basic book of the Church Study Course, the authors state: "Church organization is the way whereby members relate themselves to one another for accomplishing specific church tasks." [3] If the tasks are spiritual in nature, then the organization must be spiritual. The tasks of a church are grouped into programs, and the program determines the organization needed as a tool to help do its spiritual work.

3. *Organization as an Educational Tool*

Organization, properly conceived, does not exist for its own sake. It is a means to an end. In educational programs, organization is a vehicle for involving learners in the study of content and in related actions and experiences. This is not

---

[2] Lewis Joseph Sherrill and John Edwin Purcell, *Adult Education in the Church* (Richmond: John Knox Press, 1939), p. 141. Used by permission.

[3] W. L. Howse and W. O. Thomason, *A Church Organized and Functioning* (Nashville: Convention Press, 1963), p. 17. Used by permission.

a new concept. Early in this century an adult religious educator wrote: "Organization is only a tool; very useful in the hands of those who understand its purpose but of itself wholly helpless." [4]

A church's tasks as assigned to its organizations were stated in chapter 2, and the specific tasks of Training Union (as implemented through its courses of study) were explored in chapter 3. The Training Union organization carries out the church tasks assigned to it. The tasks, or programs, determine the organization. Organization is a tool used to accomplish church educating functions.

II. Some Elements in Organization

Organization is a part of the total curriculum for training. The curriculum includes all of the materials, activities, and experiences utilized by a training group to reach its goals.

Organization involves such elements as: *classification by congenial groups;* the *group as an instrument in learning;* and the *organizational framework*. These place each individual in position to participate actively and purposefully in the training process.

1. *Classification by Congenial Groups*

In church member training, many methods of classifying individuals into congenial groups might be used. Some have humorously suggested that adults might be grouped according to weight, height, or the amount or color of hair. Other methods have been tried. The most effective and practical method used by Southern Baptists is a classification by chronological age. Grading, as this process is commonly known, is not a new idea. It has been used as an aid in education by a variety of institutions involved in the educational process.

Classification has been described as the cornerstone of democratic education. As one educator expressed it: "Adults

---

[4] W. C. Barclay, "Organized Adult Class," *The Encyclopedia of Sunday Schools and Religious Education* (New York: Thomas Nelson & Sons, 1915), II, 747.

must be *known* before they can be *taught*. They must be classified before they can be educated." [5] Grading must be understood if it is to be accepted by adults. Acceptance is necessary if grading is to be effective.

(1) *The meaning of grading.*—Grading has been defined as "the putting together in groups the persons whom we may expect to learn well together." [6]

(2) *Some reasons for grading by age in church member training.*—In order to learn well as a group, members must be congenial; but a measure of diversity does not destroy congeniality. Grading by age has proved most effective in forming a comprehensive and workable congeniality which also includes a stimulating diversity. It would not be possible to find a basis for classification in which learners would be alike in all the factors which affect learning. The best learning situation would not be produced if such were possible because some differences "spark" the learning process. They stimulate and challenge a group to try different approaches and to entertain diverse views.

Since age determines the composite of all the interests of individuals to a greater degree than any other factor, it has become the key to classification. Age draws individual differences into a congenial unit.

People of the same age, though not all on a uniform spiritual level, do have potentialities for similar religious experiences. Spiritual truths must be given interpretation and application in terms of the characteristic experience of an age group.

Age determines best any similarities of background as related to society in general. People can be expected to have many of the same attitudes, ideas, and habits when they have all experienced changes in public school teaching theory, wars, depressions, and other significant events at similar times in their personality development.

---

[5] Earl F. Zeigler, *Toward Understanding Adults* (Philadelphia: The Westminster Press, 1942), p. 26. Used by permission.

[6] Lewis J. Sherrill, *Religious Education in the Small Church* (Philadelphia: The Westminster Press, 1932), p. 134. Used by permission.

(3) *Some advantages of grading.*—These include the following:

Proper grading will help an organization to grow.

It makes possible objective and effective administration.

It fixes responsibility for enlistment of prospects.

It prevents embarrassment and indecision on the part of new members in selecting a union.

It furnishes a fair plan for distributing prospects for growth.

It makes the organization of new units easier, and new units are a necessity for growth in an organization.

Grading emphasizes the individual and his needs.

It helps to maintain small units which are necessary for the most effective learning by individuals.

It recognizes personal growth.

It focuses on the changes and stages of development in life.

It emphasizes each period in life as distinctive and important.

Grading is democratic.

It breaks down social lines and class distinctions.

It provides congenial groups of both similar and diverse interests.

(4) *Classifying adults in Training Union.*—Classification of adults into learning units in Training Union is done on the age basis. Members are divided on this basis into departments and unions. The sexes are not separated because the Training Union is coeducational in purpose. The Training Union provides training for men and women for working together in a church. Husbands and wives are classified in the same union by grading them on the basis of the age of one partner or by arriving at a mid-age for the couple. (The mid-age is found by adding the ages of each and dividing by two.) The mid-age method makes the classification of new members and prospects somewhat more difficult, but some churches have used it effectively. The decision of how to classify husbands and wives together is a policy to be decided upon by the Training Union council of each church.

Proper classification and annual promotion must be used to keep departments and unions properly graded and to achieve the advantages of grading.

The reasons for grading and the advantages to be achieved by its proper use apply to one church as completely as to another. They are basic principles in a method of work which has been proved effective. Southern Baptists have demonstrated the value of unity in methods as well as in the value of basic unity in doctrine.

2. *The Group as an Instrument in Learning*

The group can serve as an instrument in learning. The group offers one of the most effective channels through which a church can inspire and lead individuals to experience growth toward spiritual maturity. People can experience spiritual growth best when they participate with others in learning experiences. This is indicated by current findings in group dynamics, social psychology, human relations, cultural anthropology, and administration, People grow spiritually as they work together. Refining interactions in group participation helps the group to serve as a powerful means of deepening Christian experience and motivating spiritual growth.

The concept of growth through participation in the group is upheld by authorities in fields other than religion. A psychiatrist who wrote with insight and authority observed: "Healthy growth is thought of in terms of growing forward or growing into, and is a totally integrated process through which human energy is always directed toward closer creative participation with others." [7]

Individuals themselves seem to prefer learning by groups and by participation. Adult learners want to play an active role in the learning process. In a five-year period, this preference was noted in a number of adults in this country. The majority of them responded to the demonstration-laboratory and informal group courses. Moreover, the formal lecture course showed the greatest reduction in enrolments.

Group-centered learning by participation is not only

---

[7] Alexander Reid Martin, *Recent Trends in Psychiatry of Particular Significance for Religion* (New York: Commission on Religion and Health, Federal Council of the Churches of Christ in America), p. 16.

more pleasant, but it is also "actually more productive than leader-directed groups." This was stated by the former director of the Adult Education Association of the U.S.A. He explained that the reason for this educational phenomenon is that when a group takes responsibility for its own operation, it has many more resources to use than any individual has. The group is probably a much harder taskmaster than a leader would be, and each member has a more personal interest in the success of the group.

Other religious educators who have not been acquainted with Southern Baptists' plan of Training Union work have deplored the lack of group-centered, participating programs of education in the churches. The comment of one educator was: "Religious education by group thinking is the most neglected area in the church's program. Adults know how to listen; they know little about group thinking and discussion." [8]

Another such educator and writer published an entire book. The concern of the book, *The Group Workshop Way in the Church* by Paul F. Douglass, was that the group workshop principle be put to work in the program of the churches.

These educators have recognized the value of the group as an agent in adult education. They are expressing their concern and desire for a program of work for Adults in other churches such as has been offered and proved in the Training Unions of Southern Baptist churches.

One of the characteristics of adults is that they require the right to disagree. The adult learner must have the feeling that he can express disagreement with the group if he is to contribute freely and feel a full sense of participation. The social committee can do much to help the program committee by contributing to an environment of love. Love is the Christian aid to growth through discussion. It guarantees that the person who disagrees will still be accepted, loved, and respected by the group of persons with whom he is training.

---

[8] Zeigler, *op. cit.*, p. 81.

What every human being hungers for more than anything else on earth is love. This goes for all ages. But adult love means acceptance, warmth, give-and-take, laughter, smiles, compliments, and certainly participation. It means the opportunity to express yourself in a favorable environment. It also includes the enjoyment of seeing others express themselves.[9]

3. Organizational Framework

(1) *Organization is an educational program tool.*—With organization in Training Union, people are grouped for effective training, responsibilities are assigned, direction and help are given, and involvement of all of the learners is secured.

(2) *Two organization plans are offered for adult unions.*— Adults in Training Union are offered two patterns or plans for organizing their unions. One is called the regular plan; the other is the alternate plan.

In the regular plan at least eight officers are used to secure participation of all members. A highly structured approach places people where they can be effectively involved in both groups and committees. This plan has been used profitably for over thirty years, and it continues to be recommended by the Training Union Department of the Baptist Sunday School Board.

The alternate plan was designed in 1963 after several years of research and the testing of various patterns in a large number of churches across the Southern Baptist Convention territory. It is less structured than the regular plan. It offers an approach with fewer officers, and features are kept operational. Only three to four officers are used, and there are no standing committees or groups. This is intended to simplify the administrative load of the head of the union and to decrease the size and number of the required planning team(s). The alternate plan of organization for Adult unions will be described in detail and with appropriate illustrations in chapter 5.

---

[9] R. Lofton Hudson, "Pray and Play," *Church Recreation,* (January, February, March, 1955), p. 4. Used by permission.

III. Regular Adult Union Organization

An Adult union should be organized to arrange for individual participation. Through the design of the regular plan of Adult union organization, each member can be placed in a position to participate.

1. *An Adult Union Organized*

The organization of an Adult union following the regular plan includes three elements: *officers, groups,* and *committees.* The organization chart shown on page 66 presents the arrangement of these elements. The chart is used in organizing a union. First the officers indicated are elected, and their names are placed on the chart in the designated positions. Then the other members are assigned to committees, and their names are placed in the open positions running vertically under each committee title. The groups (which run horizontally on the chart) are thus formed. Each group is under the direction of the group captain indicated. All officers, with the exception of the secretary, are responsible for directing the work of some of the other members, either on a committee or a group. The purpose of this plan is to assure participation of each member by assigning this responsibility to both his group captain and his committee chairman. The directing and supervising of several designated members also gives these officers practical training, though on a small scale, in leadership skills.

Certain responsibilities related to the tasks of Training Union are assigned to each of the committees. Because members of a committee represent different groups, each committee member is given leadership responsibility for directing the members of his group in learning the things assigned to his committee.

2. *Training Relationships Charted*

The regular plan is an interlocking type organizational pattern. Members are effectively arranged and directed both by groups and by committees. (The term "interlocking" comes from an examination of the organization chart which shows each member at a point where groups and committees interlock on the chart.) The regular plan is also designed to help all union members develop skills in participation and in the direction of, or the work with, other members in achieving goals.

ORGANIZATION CHART
(For Young People's and Adult Unions)
UNION

DUTIES OF THE COMMITTEES	PROGRAM COMMITTEE	MEMBERSHIP COMMITTEE	MISSIONARY COMMITTEE	BIBLE READING COMMITTEE	SOCIAL COMMITTEE
	1. Plan programs. 2. Assign parts in advance. 3. Lead the presentation of the programs. 4. Promote study course.	1. Check on absentees. 2. Win and instruct new members. 3. Direct visitation. 4. Encourage members to be on time. 5. Enlist members in preaching attendance. 6. Promote prayer meeting attendance.	1. Educate members in missions. 2. Lead members to be soul-winners. 3. Promote tithing and stewardship. 4. Plan missionary activities. 5. Present missionary feature in weekly meeting.	1. Conduct Bible drill. 2. Enlist members in daily Bible reading and prayer. 3. Plan for a Bible reading crusade. 4. Promote family worship.	1. Arrange room. 2. Greet and introduce visitors. 3. Put members in contact with sick. 4. Plan and conduct socials and fellowships. 5. Help in visitation program.
GROUP 1	PRESIDENT / GROUP CAPTAIN	VICE PRESIDENT	MISSIONARY LEADER	BIBLE READERS' LEADER	SOCIAL LEADER
GROUP 2	GROUP CAPTAIN				
GROUP 3	GROUP CAPTAIN				SECRETARY (Not on any Committee)

This chart may be enlarged to four groups or decreased to two groups to accommodate larger or smaller enrolments.

3. *Election of Officers Described*

The officers, with the exception of the president, are elected by the members upon the report from a union nominating committee. This nominating committee is appointed by the president. This is usually done every six months. An officer may be reelected once, therefore serving for a period of one year. At the next election the union members who may not have held an office are customarily elected. Those who have held offices are elected to other offices or placed on other committees. This procedure eventually gives training to most of the members in all of the responsibilities of the union. This helps them learn how to carry out church tasks for adults as assigned to the Training Union.

The president should be elected by the church. The union, through the department director (if there is a department organization), may submit to the church nominating committee its recommendation for a president. However, the president's position is enhanced considerably if he is elected by the church; thus, he becomes a church officer. The president is officially the contact between the church and one of its units of organization, an Adult union. He is responsible to the church for what is done in the union, and he represents the needs of the union and its members to the church.

4. *Responsibilities of Officers and Committees Assigned*

As explained earlier in this chapter, every officer and member, with the exception of the secretary, serves on one of the five committees in an Adult union using the regular organization plan.

The organization chart indicates the following committees with the designated officers serving as chairmen:

Committee	Chairman
Program	President
Membership	Vice-President
Missionary	Missionary Leader
Bible Reading	Bible Readers' Leader
Social	Social Leader

Certain responsibilities are assigned to each committee. These are part of the total curriculum of training. The chairman of each committee is assigned the leadership responsibility of directing the members of that committee. They are to train other union members in the areas assigned to their committee. Discharging this responsibility develops leadership ability in administration. The word administration is frequently misunderstood, but it is basically a spiritual ministry concept.

The ministry of administration is to direct people as a group to achieve spiritual goals.[10]

Each committee member has the assigned responsibility of leading in those areas the members of the group which he represents. Each committee is composed of a representative from each group in the union. For a detailed listing of duties of each officer, see Appendix I. A brief discussion of each committee and the responsibilities which are assigned to its chairman and members follows:

(1) *President and program committee.*—It is the responsibility of the president and group captains, who are the members of the program committee, to plan the training-study sessions in the units of the lesson courses. They are a team for detailed process planning. These officers must plan to use every member of the union in this activity of self-expression. They should plan to augment the material in the quarterlies and choose the best methods and materials for presentation. This is necessary if the interest of the union members is to be heightened.

It is also the responsibility of the program committee to lead the union members to engage in the study of textbooks in the Church Study Course. These books will deepen and broaden the interests of the members in general areas of Christian growth and in the development of specialized skills for service through their church.

---

[10] Howse and Thomason, *op. cit.;* p. 27.

(2) *Vice-president and membership committee.*—The responsibility assigned to the membership committee and its chairman, the vice-president, is that of enlisting and maintaining membership. In his book *The Local Church*, Albert W. Beaven has pointed out that "the first objective in the program of any church must be to secure people within whom its purposes may take effect."

The vice-president and members of the membership committee are responsible for leading the union members to win new members, to check on absentees, and to encourage all members to be punctual in their attendance at all of the meetings. This committee plans and directs the visitation program of the union, coordinating it with that of the general Training Union and the church.

Another responsibility of the membership committee is to enlist union members in preaching attendance and in prayer meeting attendance. They should also encourage their enlistment and full participation in the other organizations and activities of their church.

This committee also fulfils the union's responsibility in new church member orientation. It works with the church's director of new church member orientation to enlist new church members of the union's age span and to integrate them into the fellowship of training within the union.

(3) *Missionary leader and missionary committee.*—Responsibilities in some of the most vital areas of training for church members are assigned to the members of the missionary committee. This committee, led by its chairman, the missionary leader, is to train the members in soul-winning, missions, stewardship, and ministering.

This officer and the committee are to utilize every opportunity to help union members train for skills in *witnessing* effectively by using their own experience and the Bible's message of salvation. The chairman should be a soul-winner and should take each committee member on the field for in-service training. In the same manner, committee members should train each member of their respective groups. A full union of members trained to witness will be a larger number of soul-winners than the average church now has. They can lead the church to become what Christ intended—a witnessing body.

This committee is to train the members in *missions*. Members are to have a personal acquaintance and sense of participation in the mission outreach of their church and denomination in preaching, teaching, and healing both at home and around the world. They should train members to observe the Great Commission.

This committee is to guide members to understand and commit themselves to the *stewardship* of life. This includes not only the scriptural plan of tithing to support the work of the church and denomination, but it also includes the earning of money and the proper use of the other nine tenths. Stewardship of life encompasses time, talent, and influence.

It is also the responsibility of the members of the missionary committee to direct members in training activities which express practical missionary concern outside the union. These activities could take the form of conducting a devotional service in a hospital or other institution; preparing and distributing baskets of food and clothing when needed; helping in the organization of new Training Unions; establishing a program of visitation in hospitals and nursing homes; and other similar activities. Many of these activities should be planned as follow-through or applied learning of the study sessions.

A special project in the area of the missionary committee's responsibility has been developed for Training Union as part of a coordinated plan by the denomination. This is the distribution of *Home Life* magazine as a means of witnessing through the printed page. Copies can be taken to doctors' offices, barber shops, transportation waiting rooms, and other public places.

(4) *Bible readers' leader and Bible reading committee*.— The members of the Bible reading committee, including the chairman who is the Bible readers' leader, guide in the training of union members in daily, personal, and devotional reading of the Bible, as well as in family worship. The former

is done by enlisting members to participate in the Bible
Readers' Course. This is coupled with prayer for missionaries and workers in the denomination and other specific
needs for which church members should be trained to pray.
To encourage such participation and to help the members to
clearly understand the Bible's message, a weekly feature—
review, preview or test—is prepared and presented by the
leader or a committee member. Concerning these Bible reading activities, J. M. Crowe has observed:

The habit of daily regularity in Bible reading, meditation, and
prayer is established in the life of a person by the Training Union.
Perhaps nothing in the entire training program of a church does
as much to produce spiritual strength in the individual as the
use of the Bible Readers' Course and Missionary Prayer Calendar.[11]

A part of the Bible Readers' Course is designed to
develop skills in prayer. It suggests items which need prayer
and for which church members need to learn to pray.

This committee leads the union members to participate
in the Bible Reading Crusade. This is a special project to
enlist other church members who are not in Training Union
to participate in the Bible Readers' Course and Missionary
Prayer Calendar. This activity permits members to testify
outside the union concerning the individual growth benefits
of Bible study and prayer.

It is also the responsibility of the Bible reading committee to demonstrate how family worship periods can be established and maintained in each home represented.

(5) *Social leader and social committee.*—The members of
the social committee, led by the social leader, are assigned
the responsibility of helping the union to meet one of the
most basic needs of individuals. This is the need for love
and fellowship.

Maintaining the fellowship in the union is partially accom-

---

[11] J. M. Crowe, "Gaining Strength Through Training," *The Baptist
Training Union Magazine* (April, 1955), p. 8. Used by permission.

plished by the social leader and members of this committee as they serve as hosts in the union meetings. In advance of the meeting, they prepare the room so that it is comfortable, attractive, and functional. They greet visitors and members at the door, make introductions, and otherwise establish a feeling of gracious informality as a host would in his home.

To further the building of personal fellowship between members and their families, the social committee plans and conducts social activities for the union. These may be extensively planned with invitations, decorations, games, and refreshments. They may just be informal gatherings for a meal or refreshments following another union activity. The combining of social and recreational activities with those of enlistment, of some practical ministry, or of planning, can heighten the effectiveness of both.

In addition to building fellowship in the union and in social activities, the social committee seeks to deepen the feelings of love and appreciation for one another. It places members in contact with other members and prospects who have sickness or some special crisis in the family.

(6) *Secretary.*—The secretary is responsible for interpreting to union members the Eight Point Record System as a means of personal Christian growth. He collects individual record forms at each weekly meeting and compiles a union record as a means of evaluation of the union's training work. The secretary submits reports on achievement to the department or general Training Union secretary and keeps permanent and accurate records. He checks union performance against the guidance requirements of the Standard of Excellence.

The secretary, though not on any committee, serves them all. His weekly reports include one to each of the committee chairmen concerning members who have not marked items on the record system which relate to that committee's responsibilities for training the members. The secretary's work is vital in producing and maintaining an efficient organization and a high level of training proficiency for members.

CHAPTER 5

5

Additional Organizational Approaches Can Be Used

IN CHAPTER 4, the organization known as the regular plan was discussed. This chapter presents an additional organizational approach which can be used with adult unions. It is known as the alternate plan. It features a simplified and flexible approach, with fewer officers than the regular plan and no standing committees or groups. A comparison of the two plans is charted as an aid in choosing between them.

Also presented in this chapter is an organizational approach which will be needed if there is more than one adult union organized. The adult department organization is described—its function, need, grading, and officers.

I. ALTERNATE ADULT UNION ORGANIZATION

The alternate organization plan is designed to make possible its use by an Adult union although other Adult unions, even in the same department, choose to use the regular plan. Its interrelationships with other unions are not affected. Its intrarelationships reveal a division of responsibilities with church-elected supervision to accomplish task-related goals efficiently. A minimum of time and effort is required to maintain the organization itself. The chart on page 76 can be used to show these relationships.

II. ALTERNATE ADULT UNION ORGANIZATION OFFICERS

The officers in the alternate Adult union organization are relatively few in number. This can be very helpful when the members and prospects are small in number or when a new union is being organized. However, since the purposes and functions to be achieved by unions are the same, fewer officers in the alternate plan must each take more responsibility than when these duties are divided among more officers in the regular plan.

The *union leader* guides and coordinates the over-all work of the union in accomplishing the tasks of the church which have been assigned to Training Union, to encourage the spiritual development of each member, and to relate the union members and program to the total work of the church.

The *enlistment leader* maintains and enlarges the membership through enlisting and orienting new members, reaching absentees, keeping records, and promoting fellowship.

The *activities leader* leads members in activities to gain skills and to train them in witnessing, ministering, Bible reading, stewardship, and missions.

A *study leader* serves with the union leader as a planning team for the lesson course unit for which he is selected, accomplishes the detailed planning, and leads the union study-training sessions of the assigned unit.

Here is a description of the election procedure, term of office, and specific duties of the four officers.

1. *Union Leader*

The union leader should be nominated by the church nominating committee and elected for one year by the church. He may or may not be of the same age as the union's age span. Recommendations should be received by the church nominating committee from department directors or from the general director. Union members should also be given an opportunity to make suggestions of persons who could lead them effectively.

The union leader has heavy responsibilities and numerous duties. He must depend upon capable officers and willing members to function under his supervision to accept special tasks. He will, therefore, receive help in carrying the work load of the union, and he will be helping other officers and members to become involved and to develop needed skills.

ALTERNATE ADULT UNION
Organization Chart

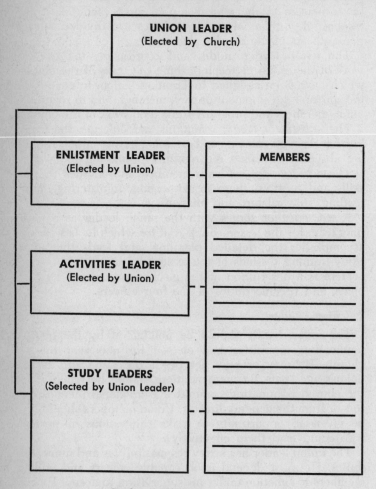

UNION LEADER
(Elected by Church)

ENLISTMENT LEADER
(Elected by Union)

ACTIVITIES LEADER
(Elected by Union)

STUDY LEADERS
(Selected by Union Leader)

MEMBERS

_____Guidance Relationship

— — — — — —Communication Relationship

The duties of the union leader are as follows:

1. To serve as administrative officer of the union, representing it in the department planning meeting. In nondepartment Training Unions, he represents the union on the Training Union council. This provides the link between the union and the church.

2. To preside over union meetings. In advance of any absences, he notifies the enlistment leader.

3. To appoint a nominating committee to recommend union-elected officers. He may also appoint other temporary committees, or individuals, for special tasks not assigned to other union officers.

4. To guide other officers in planning for all phases of union work. Arrange planning meetings as necessary. (Planning meetings are discussed in chapter 6.)

5. To orient, train, and guide all officers in their assigned responsibilities, to plan for their personal development in these assignments, and to schedule periodic evaluations of the work for which they are responsible.

6. To plan for all members to study books in the Church Study Course, to secure forms and arrange for members to complete the requirements, and request awards when earned in the Lesson Course Study Plan, Home Study Plan, or in class study. He inspires members to work toward higher recognition through advanced diplomas in the Church Study Course awards series. (See pp. viii and ix for an explanation of requirements for earning awards.)

7. To assist in the church's plan for discovering, recruiting, and training potential leaders, to indicate to the church nominating committee and the Training Union director of training those members who have leadership ability and are ready for service or for specialized leadership training.

8. To provide organization and leadership for special projects of the church, as requested, by assigning responsibilities to existing officers or by appointing short-term committees.

9. To serve as chief programing officer and to make effective utilization of the lesson courses.

(1) He leads the union each quarter in the "Unit Selection Plan" in the adult quarterlies.

(2) He selects a study leader to lead the union study of each selected unit. (It may be necessary to enlist more than one per-

son to serve as study leader for long units of 8–12 weeks.)

(3) He guides study leaders in planning and leading the units.

(4) He personally plans and directs the study of some units (at least one unit each year).

(5) He provides special training opportunities for union members who may be selected to serve as study leaders. He recommends books on the subject of learning techniques, leadership, and tools, clips articles from *The Baptist Training Union Magazine*, shares pamphlets and other materials which have been made available to the chief programing officer.

2. *Enlistment Leader*

The enlistment leader should be elected by the union for a period of six months. He is not to do all the work, but should enlist other union members to perform assignments in the area of his responsibility. He should do this frequently, making definite and specific assignments. Every member attending should complete at least one assignment monthly.

In larger unions, the enlistment leader may choose to enlist individuals to assume certain portions of his responsibilities on a continuing basis. Examples of these responsibilities are keeping records or maintaining a prospect file. If such help is enlisted for longer than a month, the persons could be designated as associate leaders for that duty. They would be responsible to the enlistment leader, who would continue to have the full responsibility to the union.

The duties of the enlistment leader are as follows:

1. To prepare plans and assignments for maintaining the membership by:
   (1) Enrolling prospects, and
   (2) Reaching absentee members.

2. To greet and present new members and visitors.

3. To assist at the union level in the church program of new church member orientation. He works with the director of new church member orientation in enrolling prospects for that program. Upon completion of the orientation, he helps lead them into union membership.

4. To maintain records and make reports on the Eight-Point

Record System. (If a union wishes to retain the office of secretary, it is recommended that this officer be considered as associate to the enlistment leader and be responsible to him.)

5. To direct efforts to publicize meetings by using announcements, posters, etc.

6. To plan union fellowship and social activities, to enlist and organize the necessary leaders for special social occasions, and to work to foster a spirit of love in which free exchange of ideas can be constructively exchanged.

7. To preside, and in other matters serve as assistant administrative officer in the absence of the union leader.

3. Activities Leader

The activities leader should be elected by the union for six months. He should not attempt to do all the work because he has a wide range of duties. He should enlist other union members to perform specific assignments in the areas of his responsibility.

Union members will decide the extra activities which are appropriate for the union. The leadership responsibility will be assigned to the activities leader, or through him to some other member. Included here are a number of duties which suggest some possible activities.

The duties of the activities leader are as follows:

1. To assist church members in establishing and improving daily worship as individuals and in family groups, as well as in congregational worship.

2. To train church members to witness. He uses testimonies, films, Scripture-marking drills, demonstration soul-winning interviews, evangelistic tracts, and assigned visits to unsaved persons for a laboratory experience in developing needed skills.

3. To train church members to minister. This includes specific opportunities in working with the needy, visiting the sick in hospitals and nursing homes, and visiting members in times of crisis.

4. To prepare Bible features to stimulate members to read the Bible daily with understanding. He leads such features in the department assembly when asked or in the union as often as agreed upon in advance planning.

5. To prepare brief features on missions and stewardship, and

to provide and interpret other information regarding the work of the church and denomination.

6. To work closely with the union leader and the study leader to recommend and develop follow-through activities which are appropriate to specific units of study. Such activities may be suggested by the union during the study-training sessions. Activities can then become logical extensions of the training which has begun in these union meetings. (They are also most appropriate opportunities to help accomplish duties 2 and 3.)

4. Study Leader

A study leader should be selected by the union leader for each unit which the union leader is not directing. Each study leader should be selected on the basis of his knowledge of the subject area and/or his interest and ability to plan and direct group study. (It may become necessary for more than one person to serve as study leader for portions of the longer units of study, e.g. those planned for 8–12 weeks in length.) Most union members will eventually serve as a study leader. In addition, there may be study leaders enlisted from outside the regular union membership when there are persons in the church with exceptional knowledge of a subject area.

The duties of a study leader are as follows:

1. To consult with the union leader for general planning of the assigned unit of study.

2. To accomplish the detailed planning and lead the union in the study of the unit.

3. To make sure that learning aids are prepared or secured, to work with the church librarian, and to provide other supplemental resources for the study.

4. To work with the union leader and the activities leader in recommending and developing follow-through activities appropriate to the unit of study.

5. To involve all members in some type of participation in the study, making at least one assignment per month.

III. Preparing to Use the Alternate Organization Plan

Since the alternate plan of organization is the newer plan, more union members are familiar with the regular plan. It seems appropriate, therefore, to offer some suggestions to unions who consider using the alternate plan. It is *not* the perfect plan, providing miracle answers to solve all existing problems. It should not be burdened with such a misconception in advance if it is later to have a chance to work effectively within its acknowledged limitations. Not all unions will want to use the alternate plan. To make a choice, a union should see the first two items below and the chart in section IV, "Comparing Adult Union Organization Plans."

1. Realize that neither the alternate nor the regular plan of organization is recommended above the other. The regular plan will be preferred by those unions that desire more structure in their organization, definite duties and instructions for each member, and involvement assured by the functioning of groups and committees. The alternate plan will be preferred by those who desire more flexibility in the planning and assigning of tasks through fewer officers to involve all members.

2. Understand that the new Adult lesson courses can be used by unions following either organization plan.

3. Explain to union members the features of both organization plans. Examine the advantages and limitations of each. Ask members to express their preference. If the choice is to use the alternate plan, proceed with Item 4.

4. Through the church nominating committee, enlist a qualified person to become the union leader and have him elected by the church. He is to serve as a church officer. His responsibility for leading the union in a continuous program of quality training requires that he have high leadership ability. (If such a leader cannot be enlisted for this major church responsibility, plans to use the alternate organization should be postponed until he can be found.)

5. Lead the union to elect the enlistment leader and the activities leader. This should be done upon report of a union nominating committee with the union leader serving as its chairman. Enter the names of these three officers and the other members on the organization chart. (The study leader's name will be added later when selected.)

6. Schedule a meeting of the officers to study and discuss duties and accept or assign specific responsibilities for planned activities.

7. Remember that adults appreciate things being done correctly; they do not want to be members of a group which operates on the "get-by" level. They respond to obvious preparation by their leaders.

To accomplish adequate preparation, the union leader will plan to meet with the officers in regularly scheduled meetings for planning and evaluation or to call meetings with the team or with the individual officers informally when necessary. (See chap. 6 for a discussion of regular and informal planning meetings.)

It is imperative that officers of the alternate organization plan together and correlate their work to insure regular involvement of every member. The concept of fewer officers and a more flexible program of work may cause officers in the alternate plan to mistakenly feel that less work is required, especially in the area of planning. This is not the case.

The regular plan is aided in its approaches to training all members by its organizational structure. The alternate plan depends more upon personal leadership and individual, specific assignments. This necessitates very careful planning.

8. Determine to follow the alternate plan for at least nine to twelve months before evaluating it for future use.

IV. COMPARING ADULT UNION ORGANIZATION PLANS

Advantages of Regular Plan	*Advantages of Alternate Plan*
1. *Older*	1. *Newer*
Has attractiveness of being better known and "proved"	Has attractiveness of "the new"
New ideas sometimes distrusted	Avoids fear of being "left behind"; provides "the latest"
	Was designed specifically to implement the tasks of Training Union
2. *More Structured*	2. *Simplified or Less Structured*
Better guarantee of involving all members with assignments, thus aiding development of members	More flexible to meet new and changing goals and to adapt organization to dif-

and contributing to regular attendance

Less chance that members will be overlooked or missed if absent

Better supervision and help for all members assured, with assignment to and leadership by both group captain and a committee chairman

ferent needs of different unions

Easier to understand and set up, especially in new unions

Less time and energy required to maintain organization

Less likelihood that maintaining organization will become an end in itself

More time available for study of content

Simpler correlation of effort

Better grouping of related activities

Can move to accomplish activities more rapidly

3. *More Officers*

Elected responsibility given to more people

Opportunity to gain skills in planning and supervision given to more church members

Less responsibility for each officer

Easier to get officers to agree to serve

3. *Fewer Officers*

Responsibility centralized

Easier to assemble a planning team

More responsibility for each officer

Easier to find fewer persons to serve as officers, especially in small unions

4. *Less Dominant Leader in President*

Leadership less centralized

4. *More Dominant Leader in Union Leader*

Leadership more centralized

Provides less opportunity for poor leader to become an obstruction

Shorter term of office

Easier to change leaders

More people given opportunity to practice administrative skills

More people qualified to serve in role with less responsibility

Sense of commitment and accountability or responsibility to church

Longer continuity of service with possibility for growing in leadership skills through training

Can keep good leaders in service with longer terms and recommended re-election

Can be more promptly decisive, moving quickly to accomplish more work

More challenging position for best leadership potential found in a church

V. The Adult Department

1. *Function of the Adult Department*

The purpose of the department organization for Adults is to set up, build, and supervise as many strong Adult unions as are needed to reach and train all adult church members. Adult departments are needed for unions using either the regular or alternate plans of organization.

Adult departments provide additional training opportunities for members before a larger group. Departments also furnish a special medium of fellowship for those who are members of the unions that comprise the department. Many people respond better to the spirit of a larger group.

2. *Number of Departments Needed*

(1) A church with sufficient adult members to have two adult unions can have an adult department. The organization of such a department can aid in establishing and building additional adult unions.

(2) A department may have from as few as two to as many as eight unions. Four is probably an ideal number for the most efficient administration.

(3) A church should have as many Adult departments in the Training Union as are needed to reach the adult membership of the church. Every resident adult church member ought to be "in training" for the work of Christ.

3. Grading of Unions and Departments

(1) Where there are multiple departments, the same age spans are recommended for Training Union as are used in the Sunday School of that church. If there are fewer departments in Training Union, a proper adjustment of the age spans should be made. In churches where there are two departments, it is generally recommended that they be designated as Adult I, approximately ages 25–39; and Adult II, approximately ages 40 and above. If a third department can be added, the ages for it could begin at approximately age 55. Due to the particular age make-up of their different constituencies, the ideal age span for departments in different churches may vary. An adjustment of the age spans will be made up and down the line as other Adult departments are provided in a growing Training Union.

(2) Unions within departments should be graded on the age basis. However, husbands and wives should be in the same union. Use the age of either the wife or husband as the key for classifying them, or use their "mid-age." (Found by adding the ages of both and dividing the sum by two.)

(3) Annual promotion should be observed between unions in the department and between departments.

VI. ADULT DEPARTMENT ORGANIZATION

1. Adult Department Organization Chart

The department director is the administrative head of this unit of organization. The department director, associate director, secretary, song leader, pianist, and president from each of the unions constitute the administrative and planning group for the department.

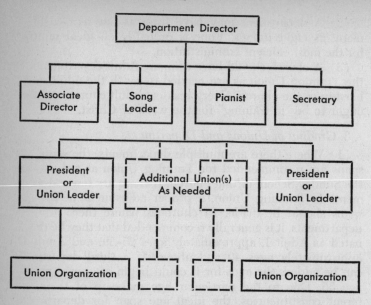

"Union Organization," as shown in the preceding chart, can be either the regular plan or the alternate plan. All unions may follow the same plan, or one or more may follow the regular plan, while others choose the alternate plan.

2. *The Department Officers*

All of the adult department officers are elected by the church. Their names are usually submitted to the church nominating committee by the Training Union director. They serve for a period of one year or for the term of other church-elected officers. They can be reelected as long as they continue to serve effectively. Their duties are listed as follows:

(1) *The department director*

Presides over all department meetings.

Works with the other department officers to plan the meetings and other work of the department.

Represents the department on the Training Union council unless the Training Union is fully organized and only division directors and other general officers serve on the council.

Makes recommendations to the church nominating committee for department officers and union leaders to be elected by the church.

Works with the director of training to discover potential leaders and to schedule training opportunities.

Serves as chief programing officer of the department, planning and leading department assembly programs or Bible features. He also leads unions to engage in their respective programing activities.

Provides organization and leadership for special projects of the church.

Provides and interprets information regarding the work of the church and denomination.

Provides opportunities for all department and union officers to be trained in performing their duties.

(2) *The associate director*

Assists the director and works with the vice-presidents or enlistment leaders of the unions in building and maintaining the membership of the department.

Provides prospect lists to officers responsible for enlistment in the unions.

Works with the director of new church member orientation in enlisting new church members for their specialized program of counseling and instruction and then for regular study and involvement in Adult unions.

Leads in activities to build fellowship in the department.

Serves as assistant administrative officer of the department, presiding in the absence of the director and representing the department on the Training Union council.

(3) *The secretary*

Interprets the Eight Point Record System as purposeful items of performance in a checklist for continuing individual church member growth.

Maintains records of the department, compiling the weekly report to the Training Union secretary and the monthly report to the Training Union council.

Secures proper record forms for use in the department and unions.

Works with union secretaries or enlistment leaders, helping them to develop skills in maintaining and submitting permanent records.

Checks the records of the department and union against requirements of Standards of Excellence each quarter. He is responsible for seeing that requests for awards are passed from the department director to the general director of the Training Union for proper certification.

(4) *The song leader*

Selects music and leads singing for each department meeting. (See the Adult section of *The Baptist Training Union Magazine* for weekly suggestions in "Adult Assembly Programs.")

Arranges for special music as needed.

Endeavors to provide the department meeting place with good songbooks.

Distributes books and arranges music with pianist.

Trains an assistant by giving him instruction in conducting techniques and the opportunity to lead occasionally.

Utilizes opportunities to develop skills as song leader by appropriating training opportunities provided by church music ministry.

Serves as a member or officer in one of the unions.

Secures and uses appropriate helps.

(5) *The pianist*

Plays for all the meetings of the department.

Distributes books and plans the schedule with the song leader.

Attends the general Training Union planning meeting and department executive committee meeting.

Utilizes opportunities for additional training through the church Music Ministry.

Develops an assistant, asking him to play occasionally,

Serves as a member or officer of an adult union in the department.

Secures and uses appropriate helps.

CHAPTER 6

I. VALUES OF PLANNING

II. MAKING PLANNING SUCCESSFUL
1. Elements in Successful Planning
2. Time for Successful Planning

III. UNIT PLANNING
1. Goal Planning
2. Process Planning
3. Skills Developed Through Planning

IV. REGULAR TRAINING UNION PLANNING MEETINGS
1. The Church Council
2. The Training Union Council
3. The General Planning Meeting

V. PLANNING OUTSIDE THE PLANNING MEETINGS
1. Preplanning
2. Postplanning

6

Planning for Training Adults
Is Required

ANY PROJECT can be expected to succeed or to fail in proportion to the preparation given it. Preparation begins with planning. Planning is necessary. Yet, perhaps no other activity is more universally *praised* and less *practiced*.

One reason we do not plan—or at least delay planning past effective performance dates—is the burdensome prospect of planning. We need to see what planning is; to see that it can be divided into work assignments which represent the task in a less awesome light; and to learn to approach its accomplishment in parts, or easier segments.

Training cannot be adequately planned or undertaken until the specific tasks have been defined in terms of group and group member skills. The particular skill or ability determines the (special) knowledge, skills, and levels of skills which training should assist groups and persons to acquire. Planning the training program requires the isolation of the specific tasks for which training is to be offered.[1]

Definition of Planning

Planning is: (1) looking ahead, (2) anticipating events, and (3) deciding how to handle them.

Planning involves seeing where you are, then deciding where you want to go. It may mean, however, working backward from the intended goal to see what events and contingencies must be recognized and accomplished before the planner knows how and where to start.

[1] W. L. Howse, "The Training Concept in Training Union," (Unpublished study paper, Baptist Sunday School Board), p. 1.

Who Does Planning?

The planning group or team, to be effective, should probably not number more than eight persons.

Varying numbers of planners are recommended, however, for different types of planning. There are some learning goal decisions which are best shared by all the group participants. There are other decisions and planning process details which can best be considered by a smaller planning team. (See p. 97 for designations of those who should comprise planning teams.)

When decisions about plans are shared by all the participants, they are more likely to be practical, reachable, and therefore, more readily accomplished. But prior to, and after, such decisions by the total group, the smaller planning team has to use the best evidence it can pool to make many decisions. Administrative decisions, for the most part, must be made by the director, union leader, or president. Some decisions regarding training content and activities are also made by these church-elected leaders following church or Training Union council decisions.

I. Values of Planning

There are practical necessities which require planning. There are also other benefits which accompany planning.

Planning:

Helps things to be viewed not only as they are, but as they may become

Provides the bridge on paper between the desire to see something done and its final accomplishment

Makes flexibility possible, by identifying problems in advance and deciding how to deal with them, or postpone them

Overcomes procrastination—a primary hindrance to initiating action—by dividing large tasks into smaller ones

Capitalizes on developments—following through on successful plans, or offering substitute plans

Reduces the number of problems by putting solutions into effect before foreseen problems actually develop

Increases the supply of ideas for solving problems through the stimulus of writing them down and seeing thoughts on paper

Facilitates the assignment of responsibilities to do more work

Involves more people in the joy of participation

Gives the satisfaction of seeing plans being accomplished—recognition of "getting somewhere"

Strengthens leaders with a sense of security, cutting down on leadership casualties through resignation or failure

Makes the difference between ordinary leadership and excellent leadership.

The process of planning is good training in a society geared to run by committees and small groups. It provides excellent training in developing leadership skills necessary for effective work in churches. Planning becomes even more important here, where "snap" decisions cannot be enforced by management authority. In churches there must be persons who will lead volunteer church workers to commitment. They must be helped to understand and to become involved. Leaders can achieve this best through planning.

II. Making Planning Successful

1. *Elements in Successful Planning*

Several factors are vital to the success of any regular planning meeting. The following factors have been adapted from the Training Union section of the *Church Program Guidebook, 1965-66.*

Prayer

Preplanning by director or leader

Beginning and closing meetings on time

Conducting the meeting democratically, making sure each member feels free to express himself

Sticking with the agenda when agreed upon, after asking planning team members to suggest items in advance

Making the time count and giving priority to those items which are most important

Keeping accurate minutes of the meeting

Cultivating a spirit of optimism and enthusiasm

Following through carefully between regular meetings to assure a high standard of work.

The workers can follow a leader when they are convinced that he knows what he is doing and why. These planning sessions afford excellent opportunities for developing this assurance. Frequently, the agenda should include instruction in the Training Union tasks, methods, and administrative and training techniques.

2. Time for Successful Planning

It is agreed that planning is a practical necessity, and that it can be divided into smaller work assignments. Planning also offers abundant and recognized values. The question which overshadows the others in practical consideration, however, is the consideration of *time*.

Time is precious and seems more scarce each year in the lives of active adults. But time adequately spent in planning for a program of training will prove to be an economy expenditure. *People will find time to do the things which they consider to be important.* Thus, they give priority to their vocations, health care, social relationships, and other values which they recognize. Learning and skill development can be recognized among these values.

One authority in teaching has said: "In general, far too little time is usually budgeted for assessment and planning. One rule of thumb is: 'It takes at least a day to plan a day.'" [2]

It will take at least an hour to plan an hour. However, this cannot be applied as a weekly time schedule. Planning is a continuing activity. It is done at many times by many people in many ways. Not all planning will be done in formal planning sessions. Much of the planning for adult departments and unions in Training Union will be done in "spare-change time"—time grabbed on the run. This can be time sandwiched between other scheduled meetings, or hooked on like a trailer behind them. Such planning can be done by two or three persons sitting in a car outside the church building during a children's choir rehearsal, or si-

[2] Matthew B. Miles, *Learning to Work in Groups, A Program Guide for Educational Leaders* (New York: Bureau of Publications, Teachers' College, Columbia University, 1959) p. 60. Used by permission.

multaneously with some other meeting in which the planners are not involved, or having coffee or lunch together during a break in a day of shopping.

Some planning decisions may be made by the group in only thirty seconds, but will require thirty minutes to write down later. This type planning will require more preplanning by the planning leader to be effective. But the circumstances of busy church workers who have a flexible approach to planning and who carry multiple responsibilities are recognized.

Of course, not all planning can be done informally. There must also be a schedule of regularly planned and anticipated planning meetings.

III. Unit Planning

Goal planning and *process* planning are the two kinds of planning for units of study which will be considered. With each kind of planning, it should be helpful to describe: What generally is to be considered; *when* it is to be done; *who* is involved; and *how* it can be accomplished.

1. *Goal Planning*

What—considers the aim, or what the union chooses to learn or train for during the quarter.

When—suggests the first Sunday night union meeting of each quarter. This can be earlier by using the digests of the units. The digests are in *The Baptist Training Union Magazine* and in the Adult Group Training Guides for the preceding quarter, allowing more advanced consideration.

Who—involves as many as possible of those who are to be in the learning group—in this case, the entire union. A Sunday night union meeting is suggested because it is difficult to get as many members together at any other time.

How—recommends following the procedure given in the Group Training Guide under "Unit Selection Plan." This procedure for Sunday night should also include some prior actions by the union leader or president, such as making assignments to union members for reading the units in the quarterlies to be considered, or studying the digests given in *The Baptist Training Union Magazine* or in the previous quarter's Group Training Guide. Available resource units, which have not been studied by the union, should also be considered, along with the units presented in the quarterlies.

(1) *Unit Selection Plan procedure.*—The procedure outlined in the quarterlies will usually follow an outline similar to the following one with some variation from quarter to quarter to avoid repetition.

a. Ask members who have studied assigned units to report.—(The union members will be aided in remembering the content of presentations if posters, charts, or other visual learning aids are used.) Each will ask:

What is the theme of the unit?

How does the unit relate to current needs of our church or community? What training skills need to be developed? What actions may need to be taken?

How can the study of this unit help to meet needs of our members and prospects?

What are some of the suggestions offered by the writer to answer the problem of the unit?

b. Lead the union in open discussion of the relative merits of each unit.—Freedom to agree and disagree must be maintained, as well as keeping order in the discussion. Each member of the union should be encouraged to express himself. A high priority factor in selecting units should be the needs of the church at that time, and how members can train to do their church's work. Suggestions concerning the church's needs from the pastor or other church leaders should be relayed to the union.

c. Poll the group for its decision.—This often can be done by recognizing the general preferences expressed by the group, presenting what seems to be the consensus, and asking approval or disapproval. At other times a hand or voice vote is necessary. Frequently, a ballot is preferred. On a ballot each member suggests the units he feels are best to be studied, in the order of his preference. Units receiving the most "first preference" votes would be studied, along with the second and third choices, if the units are short enough to have three units included in one quarter's studies.

d. *Prepare a display chart showing units selected.*—List the units to be studied during the quarter, indicating the dates and the study leader or group captain for each. Add the material which should be read by the union members prior to each session when this has been determined by the study leader or group captain.

A copy of this chart should be mailed to each member.

(2) *Benefits of the Unit Selection Plan.*—The Unit Selection Plan offers the members of the union the opportunity to select from a number of units each quarter. They can choose those units which the entire union comes to feel can best meet their needs and those of the church at that time. As the members state the possible reasons for using each unit and agree on the units which will be used, they will have taken a step toward accepting group goals for learning.

As members of the union discuss the reasons or values in using certain units, and persuade one another concerning the appropriateness of these proposed learning goals, they stimulate themselves into a desire to participate in that study.

It is well to remember the principle that the adult learner learns best when he has a voice in what he is going to learn; and that group learning is an effective approach to learning—a unique approach which brings in the complementing, or "group contributing," approach to problem-solving. In this case, the problem will be, "What shall we learn?"

2. *Process Planning*

After the goal planning for study is accomplished, there is then a more involved planning approach by a smaller team.

When the unit selection procedure has been completed, the president (in the regular organization) will assign the selected units to the group captains for detailed planning. Group captains may each take responsibility for an entire unit, or they may work together, alternating the responsibility of leading each session. Union leaders (in the alternate organization) will select study leaders for the selected units and assign such responsibilities to them.

What—considers the question, How are we going to get there? It is something like the planning of a trip. Goal planning would be deciding where to go on a vacation. Process planning would involve deciding how to get to the desired destination.

When—suggests at regularly stated times, such as a monthly general Training Union planning meeting, or in special conferences on specific details of planning—such as the union leader visiting or calling the study leader (or the president calling a group captain) to discuss a method or the ordering of a learning aid.

Who—involves as few members as necessary in the details of process planning. Planning teams should include:

In the regular organization: *basic team*—president and group captains; *comprehensive team*—add other officers.

In the alternate organization: *basic team*—union leader and study leader; *comprehensive team*—add other officers.

PLANNING TEAMS

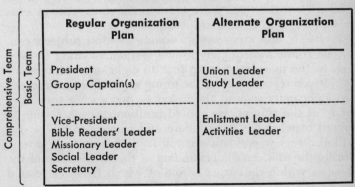

	Regular Organization Plan	Alternate Organization Plan
Basic Team	President Group Captain(s)	Union Leader Study Leader
Comprehensive Team	Vice-President Bible Readers' Leader Missionary Leader Social Leader Secretary	Enlistment Leader Activities Leader

How—includes the "Guides in Planning for Learning" which are listed here. Each of these items should be given attention in the process planning of all sessions in a unit.

(1) *Guides in planning for learning.*—Plans for individual training sessions from the quarterlies may include a number of elements. Suggested detailed plans for each session are given in the Group Training Guides under the title, "Training Procedures."

A basic outline for planning all sessions is provided in the "Guides in Planning for Learning," which have been developed by the Training Union Department.

a. Determine appropriate aim.—One of the most important steps in planning is the selection of an aim. An aim, or learning goal, is needed to give purpose and direction to the entire discussion. It also provides a worthy basis for evaluating the results of learning. A suggested aim can be found in the form of the question which appears in the quarterly at the beginning of each week's article.

The primary purpose of restating the aim is to stimulate thought and to help the planning team to adapt the study materials to the specific situation and training needs of that union in that church at that time. Basic teams, or group captains and study leaders, will want to consider very carefully the union members' needs which may be met during exploration of a given subject. They must give special attention to possible skills which members should develop in the study. Then they will work out specific statements of aims in keeping with those considerations.

b. Relate unit and session emphases.—Most subjects cannot be studied adequately in one session. Relating the session to the unit (containing four to eight or even as many as thirteen sessions) gives the group captain or study leader an opportunity to lead the union in previewing the entire study of the subject. He should positionize each session in regard to what has gone before and what is to follow. He will also review previous sessions studied from time to time during the unit. An understanding of the relationship of the sessions within the larger whole of which they are related parts, will provide needed light for planning each session and the entire unit. The relating of the session emphasis to the unit provides a bridge between the topics of the sessions, helping to establish the continuity of study necessary to satisfying learning.

c. *Select learning methods.*—The next item in planning is the selection of effective methods. It is usually found to be profitable to use more than one method or a combination of methods. Some variety in methods used is also desirable. Certainly the method of "giving parts"—or the *symposium*— is an excellent method. It should not be used, however, to the exclusion of many other good methods, such as panels, drama, buzz groups, interviews, research-reports, debate, role playing, and group discussion.

All of these methods, and others, are recommended from time to time in the specific dated suggestions in the Group Training Guides as "Training Procedures." Built into these suggestions are procedures which will help to make the union meeting a laboratory for in-service church member training. An excellent presentation of some valuable methods is included in *A Primer for Teachers and Leaders* by LeRoy Ford.

d. *Secure suitable learning aids.*—A very profitable addition to most learning situations in Training Union can be made with learning aids. Most of these aids are of the visual and/or audio variety—including many types of charts and posters, picture sets, recordings, resource kits, slides, film-strips, and the like. Many of these, such as charts, or tear sheets on newsprint, can be prepared by union members. Other learning aids and curriculum supplements are suggested, and some included, in the Group Training Guides. A number of such special learning devices are also prepared for specific units. They are available from the Church Literature Department of the Baptist Sunday School Board. These may be ordered along with the lesson course quarterlies.

A Primer for Teachers and Leaders and *Tools for Teaching and Training* by LeRoy Ford are suggested as continuing, or undated, sources for ideas in preparing appropriate learning aids. The first book includes a section on this subject, while the latter title addresses itself almost exclusively to this area. In planning, the programing team should first consult the bibliography section in the Group Training Guides for a listing of items which may be secured. These lists are usually included at the beginning of the quarterlies in order that needed items may be noted and located or ordered early enough to be received in time for the scheduled study.

Learning aids can help to speed up the learning process. They are also most helpful in maintaining or heightening the interest level of the group. This becomes especially needful during the study of the longer units when initial subject interest by a group tends to wane after several weeks.

e. Plan for follow-through activities.—A number of schools of educational thought hold that no real learning is accomplished until the learners do something to "use" that which they have studied. Certainly learning is greatly increased if the study leads to and includes application through follow-through activities. For example, a study on how to minister could be accompanied by planned visits of members to hospital wards and nursing homes. A study on witnessing could incorporate assigned visits to unsaved prospects and report-testimonies, making it a laboratory or in-service training approach for skill development. Most union activities will have heightened purpose if they flow logically from the subjects being studied.

f. Evaluate results.—Evaluation attempts to determine whether or not, or how much, the members have learned of what they "aimed" to learn. There are a number of devices for evaluating various aspects of the learning accomplished. Simple tests can be devised to measure the amount of knowledge acquired, and post-testing compared with pretesting can reveal quantitative improvement. Choosing patterns of action following case studies, or evaluating suggested solutions of hypothetical problems, or interpretations of selected pictures, can reveal changes in attitudes. These are but examples.

Other items such as participation in the discussions, or resulting activities, should be evaluated. The regular "Training Procedures" in the Group Training Guides provide helpful specific suggestions for evaluating results of lessons and units. These guides, along with *The Baptist Training Union Magazine* and *Church Administration* magazine also offer selected articles on evaluating learning.

(2) *Training-study session planning form.*—As an aid for use in planning, the following form is offered as a suggestion. It incorporates the six guides in planning for learning which have just been described. It uses the question form, which requires an answer, rather than the statement approach. Forms such as this are not available in print. Copies could be duplicated to provide a supply in a church, or this one could be used as an outline, to be followed or adapted by each planning team.

Suggested Training-Study Session or Unit Planning Form

1. What do union members want to learn or what skills need to be developed in this study? _____
   _____

2. How can union members be helped to see this session as a related part of a unit study, rather than as a separate "program"? _____
   _____

3. Which learning methods will likely be most effective?
   _____
   _____

4. What learning aids are needed? _____
   _____
   _____

5. What follow-through activities logically could apply the results of training or continue the learning? _____
   _____
   _____

6. How can the effectiveness of the training be evaluated?
   _____
   _____

3. Skills Developed Through Planning

The guides in planning for learning should aid in training workers by developing a number of skills. Some of these skills are: (1) *creativity*, by projecting thoughts ahead to visualize probable outcomes; (2) *selectivity*, by choosing from an array of good goals, methods, aids and activities to center on the best and most practical; (3) *utilization*, by applying these prepared guides to the possibilities and limitations of the union situation; (4) *communication*, by interpreting planning concepts; and (5) *evaluation*, by weighing objectively the results achieved in performance.

IV. REGULAR TRAINING UNION PLANNING MEETINGS

Union planning must be understood in relation to the total planning effort for Training Union. Union planning should be correlated with planning done throughout the organization and the church. Regular planning meetings recommended for a church are described. These meetings can be considered as administrative planning meetings, although some process planning for lesson course studies can logically be accomplished in the union section of the Training Union general planning meeting each month.

1. The Church Council

If a church has a functioning church council, Training Union planning begins with the council. The council is composed of the church staff and elected leaders of the Training Union, Sunday School, Music Ministry, Brotherhood, and Woman's Missionary Union programs. The chairman of deacons, along with some church committee chairmen, may be included. The council is usually led by the pastor and meets monthly or as needed.

The church council plans, coordinates, and evaluates the church's work.

The Training Union director represents the Training Union on the church council. He has the major responsibility for assuring members that the church has a comprehensive, balanced, and effective continuing training program.

2. *The Training Union Council*

Planning continues in the Training Union council. This first planning group in the Training Union was formerly called the Training Union executive committee.

The purpose of the Training Union council is to plan, coordinate, and evaluate the Training Union program of work —its studies, projects, and emphases. In many churches, the Training Union council is composed of all general officers in the Training Union, the adult leaders of all department units of organization, along with age group coordinators if the Training Union has these officers. (If the Training Union is fully organized with divisions of new church member orientation, church member training, and church leader training, the Training Union council may be composed of the directors of these divisions and other general officers.) In nondepartment Training Unions, adult leaders of all the unions, Junior through Adult, would be on the council.

The council should meet about the middle of each month several days prior to the Training Union general planning meeting. Short weekly meetings also have proved a valuable aid in producing consistently better work in churches which scheduled them.

The Training Union council's work can be summarized as dealing with internal *policies, plans,* and *problems* of this organization.

The council should agree upon general *policies* for the entire Training Union, such as the time schedule, grading system, and procedure for classifying members and prospects. Agreeing on policies can be called the settling of problems in advance.

The Training Union council *plans* general activities, emphases, and projects of the entire Training Union. It also approves plans of departments and unions when these need to be correlated with the general Training Union program, or given calendar time or budget. Plans for church study courses, other special training groups, annual promotion, and officers to be recommended to the church nominating committee are examples of the types of planning done by this group. Any plans which members, unions, or departments feel should be undertaken in the church, and which are encompassed in the tasks of Training Union, should be referred to this planning group.

Problems are considered as they arise and are referred to the Training Union council. Problems should be looked upon as opportunities for improving the work. Problems are evidences of a busy, working organization. This organization is composed of a number of units staffed by average people of individual differences, most of whom are volunteer leaders.

Lack of progress toward stated training goals by the Training Union, or by individual units of the organization, is a problem which should be given consideration.

Examples of other problems considered by the council could relate to discipline, meeting places, improper grading or classification of members and prospects, ineffective leaders, unions failing to use appropriate resource materials or personnel for studies, dismissal of some unions or choir members prior to scheduled time.

Frequently, when a problem is successfully handled, a policy is born.

3. *The General Planning Meeting*

Training Union detailed planning continues in the general planning meeting. This meeting was formerly called the Training Union officers' council.

Among those who attend the general planning meeting are department officers and officers of Adult unions.

The general planning meeting should be conducted about the twentieth of each month. The work of the Training Union for the past calendar month should be reviewed and plans should be made for the work of the next month.

The general planning meeting schedule may be divided into two or three periods, depending on whether the Training Union is departmentalized.

(1) *The first period.*—This is the general session, presided over by the Training Union director. If this is a supper meeting, this period could take place around the table. Plans which were made in the Training Union council would be presented. Promotional matters and special features (such as learning aids to be ordered and other resource materials available in the church library) would be presented.

(2) *The second period.*—Following the general session, officers go to their respective departments for department planning. The department directors should preside. The work of the department, generally, will be discussed; reports from union leaders or presidents should be received; and any emphases presented in the general session, or being planned within the department, should be given explanation and implementation.

This meeting is a short one of perhaps fifteen minutes. However, it is most valuable in coordinating the work of the unions and in building a spirit of fellowship. This is especially important as the size of the church increases. It becomes difficult to be very close to all the members. Members can share concerns, achievements, prayer requests, and social activities.

Of special consideration should be a decision at this time concerning if and when Bible features are to be substituted for other type assembly programs, and assignments of responsibility made to unions.

(3) *The third period.*—This session of the general planning meeting should be for union planning. Officers from each union will meet in their regular meeting place and plan the work for the next month. This includes process planning, focusing first upon the content of the lesson or training materials. Coordinating plans for enlistment, publicity, and activities with the subject areas of the lesson courses is done where possible. There will, of course, be other plans to be made by the officers. The regular business of the union should be considered, and reports should be received by the union leader or president from the other officers. Plans should be reported for things to be done dur-

ing the next month; e.g. socials, visitation, Bible features, and so on.

Consideration should be given at this time to plans for cooperating with department and general Training Union emphases, with assignments made to officers for accomplishing that which is the responsibility of the union. The church calendar should be checked for events where the union could implement or correlate efforts.

(NOTE—During the union meetings, the department officers should also meet. Generally, these officers will deal with plans for enlargement, checking Standards of Excellence performance, assignment of prospects, and the planning of department assemblies.)

V. PLANNING OUTSIDE THE PLANNING MEETINGS

1. *Preplanning*

The success of planning meetings is determined by the amount and kind of preplanning accomplished before the scheduled meeting and by the detailed planning accomplished afterwards. Individual planning should be done in advance of all the meetings. Leaders should come with ideas, tentative plans, suggestions, and questions. After polling individuals who are to be present, the leader should prepare an agenda concerning things which should be considered. The group then, following the agenda, will take the individual officers' preplanned suggestions, and discuss, refine, and develop them through the process of group interaction.

2. *Postplanning*

Much of the planning by individuals in small groups will be done after regular planning meetings. Individuals will have to consider assignments and outline their own plans for accomplishing them. There will be a great deal of person-to-person planning over the telephone and in short moments of time when two persons or a small group or committee can get together.

Other possibilities for postplanning may be short meetings before or after other church meetings, or during some of the usually varied schedules of Wednesday evening. Perhaps such planning could be done in homes, at coffee breaks, during drop-by visits, or at work. If people are convinced of the need for planning and are stimulated by practical considerations to accomplish it, they will usually motivate themselves and find the time to accomplish necessary planning.

CHAPTER 7

7

Meeting for Training Adults
Is Profitable

ALTHOUGH MEETINGS have become a much-maligned item in modern society, some writers and educators defend them. Paul F. Douglass has quoted from an interview with John R. Mott:

> Over the decades I have developed deep convictions about the power of meetings to change personal lives and to change the world. There is power in the process of thinking common problems through together, participating in planning programs of action, and performing assignments under the motivation of high spiritual mission. From my experience I have come to look upon the meeting as a superlatively social invention for human communication, and sharing of social purposes, getting work done, and—note this—for changing one's self, others, and the world.[1]

There is a reason for meetings. They have purpose and value in achieving training-learning goals.

With the foregoing definition and explanation of meetings and their function in mind, recall the discussion in the previous chapter of the three regular planning meetings. These should be kept in mind for a comprehensive study of meetings. In this chapter, attention is given to two meetings which are conducted weekly by Adult unions and departments.

I. SUNDAY NIGHT MEETINGS

Two regular meetings for adults in Training Union are usually conducted each Sunday night: the department as-

---

[1] Paul F. Douglass, *The Group Workshop Way in the Church* (New York: Association Press, 1956), p. ix. Used by permission.

sembly, where there is an Adult department organization, and the union meeting.

1. *Department Assembly*

The Adult department meets each week for a devotional and promotional period. The unions within the department come together at the beginning of the Sunday evening schedule for approximately fifteen minutes. This period includes music, prayer, Bible reading, and devotional thoughts—all accomplished in the atmosphere of close Christian fellowship which should characterize an Adult department.

The department director finds specific help for this meeting in the "Assembly Programs" in the Adult section of each issue of *The Baptist Training Union Magazine.*

If unions desire more time in their union meetings, the Bible features may be presented in the department assembly rather than in the union meeting. The Bible feature would replace any other type of assembly program. These features are also provided in the Adult section of *The Baptist Training Union Magazine.* The person responsible for the Bible feature in each union can alternate in leading this feature in the department, or it can be led by the department director.

In addition to the worship or Bible feature, the department assembly is used for promotion. "Promotion" is not a word which should stir negative feelings. It has been defined as "the procedure of distributing as widely and persuasively as possible those truths which it is to your advantage to make known." [2] "Promotion" is most appropriate in this meeting, for it is needed to accomplish goals. These goals are spiritual in nature. To accomplish its goals, a church must "distribute" or "provide and interpret information regarding the work of the church and the denomination" to all the members. Therefore, promotion—like organization—can become a tool for achieving spiritual results.

An Adult department in the Training Union is a unit of

---

[2] Nicholas Sanstag, *Persuasion for Profit* (Norman: University of Oklahoma Press, 1957), p. 3.

the church's life which lends itself well to accomplishing this interpretation, or promotion, toward spiritual results. Enthusiastic sharing of plans to accomplish needed work should be given by the department director or other officers responsible for specific areas.

Another feature of the department assembly which should not be overlooked is the opportunity for building fellowship. This church unit, where husbands and wives are together in the company of other husbands and wives and unmarried men and women, can do much to foster the love which should characterize a church. The department assembly can be a time for sharing prayer requests, for giving out good news and coming events in the lives of the members and their families, and for commending accomplishments of members. These times of sharing provide opportunities for practicing the qualities of good friendship plus the ministry of Christian love and concern. There is need for a practice of these things always. As our churches become larger and schedules more pressed, there is danger that this function will be overlooked or underexercised.

2. Union Meeting

The weekly meeting of an Adult union is ordinarily held on Sunday evening preceding the preaching service. It usually follows an assembly of the department or is followed by a general assembly of the Training Union in the church. Although much of the planning and the other training activities of the union are carried on during the week, the focus of the work of an Adult union comes at this weekly meeting. Here the records are taken, visitors are introduced, new members are received, and all members have an opportunity to participate.

It is at this meeting that the Bible feature, missionary feature, and other activities of like nature are presented. It is when the study or training session is conducted—the heart of Adult union work. This is the time when the principle of developing church member skills through individual participation is given its chief opportunity. At least fifty minutes should be given to this meeting. An outline which shows a suggested schedule for the elements of the weekly meeting is included here, both for the unions using the regular organization plan and the alternate organization plan.

The suggested schedules for the weekly meeting of a union are not meant to be restrictive. A union may wish to engage in other activities, or it may find it unnecessary to engage in all of these items each week. The schedules are

---

SUGGESTED ADULT UNION SCHEDULE
(Regular Organization Plan)

President presiding
1. Prayer
2. Opening period (10 minutes)
   Secure records
   Make announcements
   Have committee reports (1 minute each)
      Social—Brief report and recognition of visitors
      Membership—Brief report and presentation of new members
      Program—Group captain in charge of next week's training gives brief preview
      Missionary—Brief report *
      Bible reading—Brief report *
3. Bible feature (6 minutes) **—Bible readers' leader
4. Missionary feature (3 minutes)—Missionary leader
5. Secretary's report (1 minute)
6. Training-study period (30 minutes)—Group captain
   (A period of open discussion and application should frequently come at the close of the session, with follow-through activities suggested when appropriate.)
7. Prayer for evening preaching service

---

* These two committees may prefer to report in connection with their features suggested in points 3 and 4.

** See explanation under "Department Assembly" for optional plan of conducting this feature at that time.

SUGGESTED ADULT UNION SCHEDULE
(Alternate Organization Plan)

Union leader presiding

Have record forms collected at the door of the union room, having had them distributed prior to the department assembly, if the union is a part of a department organization.

1. Prayer
2. Opening period
   (1) Enlistment leader presents visitors and new members and makes visitation assignments for the week.
   (2) Activities leader makes any necessary reports and assignments concerning tasks assigned to him, other than follow-through activities on the unit study.
3. Bible feature *

On the Sundays agreed upon by the union, the activities leader, or one designated by him, presents a brief feature (5-6 minute maximum) designed to stimulate members to read the Bible daily and with understanding.

4. Training-study period—study leader or union leader in charge
   (1) Participation in training-learning activities
   (2) Assignment of any needed follow-through activities
5. Report on records
6. Prayer for the evening preaching service

---

* See explanation under "Department Assembly" for optional plan of conducting this feature at that time.

offered, however, in order that the officer planning and presiding can conduct the meeting with dispatch. It should be evident that there is a plan and a purpose to make good use of the time being invested by all members present and that the major portion of the time will be given to the most important items.

As shown by the suggested time schedules, the training-study period, when the content for training is handled, deserves major emphasis. Of course, that previous portion of the meeting where the officers report and engage upon their other duties can be considered as skill practice or in-service leadership training. The majority of the skills in the performance of church membership functions, however, must be based first upon the sharing of content.

II. OTHER POSSIBLE MEETING TIMES

In addition to the regular meetings of the church's training agency, mention should be made of other meeting times which are possible. Adult church member training is not to be confined to meetings on Sunday nights at the church.

1. Group Studies

There are groups within a church which meet with regularity at times other than on Sunday for training.

The new church member orientation classes meet at times to be decided by the church and the group's teacher or counselor—usually on Sunday evenings, Wednesday nights, and perhaps Sunday mornings during Sunday School.

Training groups for potential leaders and for specialized leaders also meet, usually at other times during the weekly schedule of a church. These groups can meet when there are scheduled meetings of organizations, such as Wednesday nights and Sunday morning, in addition to other week nights or Saturdays, depending upon the time available and the interest of the groups.

There are groups who organize themselves around a special subject interest. Frequently, this is an extension of study of a subject which began in a Training Union unit. Special interest by a number of members, frequently in different unions, develops to the point that they desire to band themselves for more intensive and extensive depth study in a subject which they have not been able to explore sufficiently in the scheduled time available in regular union meetings. These groups frequently meet on week nights, often in the homes of group members. At times, there develops a sufficient interest to organize a study group of people who are not already in a meeting during the Sunday School teachers and officers' meeting on Wednesday nights at the church.

A series of nights during a week has been used successfully for many years as special group study times in classwork appropriate to the Church Study Course. These weeks of study are ordinarily scheduled by the church council and are sponsored by church program organizations. These include January Bible Study Week and Preparation Week by the Sunday School; Church Membership Training Week by the Training Union; Music Expansion Week by the Music Ministry; and Weeks of Prayer and Study by the Woman's Missionary Union.

Retreats have become very profitable and pleasant approaches to study, training, and planning. These are meetings which take on a new dimension by transferring the group from the ordinary or usual settings. A principle of adult learning is that the learner learns best when he is happy and feels well. Pleasant surroundings and the unhurried atmosphere of a retreat make possible stimulating and satisfying training experiences enhanced by fellowship.

Informal planning times (times when small groups get together, upon call to accomplish specific objectives) constitute some of the most profitable meetings in which church members engage. These do not have to be scheduled in the church calendar; they do not require supportive meetings of younger age groups to accommodate the children; they do not have to claim more time than is required to do the job; they have the advantage of being oriented to needs. This latter characteristic is very helpful in getting the required persons to attend. Absences of key personnel frequently hampers the training and planning of groups that meet regularly on a weekly basis simply because it is the scheduled time for a meeting.

2. Socials and Fellowships

Much has already been said in this book concerning the contribution of fellowship to enlistment and learning and training activities. Christian love adds a priceless ingredient to all occasions which involve church members. It is divinely intended nourishment for Christian growth in all areas.

Socials are time-honored meetings of proved profit for individuals, units of organization, and the church in general. These meetings can take the form of planned occasions where committees are assigned responsibilities for the planning, the invitations, the decorations, the games, the refreshments, and other details. A completely planned social occasion is included for each age group, Junior through Adult, in *The Baptist Training Union Magazine* each month. *Church Recreation* magazine also provides resource materials to aid in these and other social and fellowship occasions.

Officers elected in the unions are frequently asked to provide fellowship periods in connection with other occasions such as a brief social gathering for reports and refreshments following visitation. Planning meetings can often be accompanied by a meal or followed by refreshments, especially when these are in a home or at some place other than the church. Study courses have long been enhanced, both in learning and attendance, by serving snack meals prior to, or refreshments following, class sessions.

Since eating is a necessity and is generally a pleasant experience, most Baptist groups continue to follow the example used even by Jesus. He frequently arranged opportunities for meals with those whom he wanted to teach and to train.

III. Leading Groups in Meetings

The burden lies on the leaders for making meetings for training profitable. Even in a group-centered approach, as used in an Adult union, it is the leader who has the greatest opportunity to make the gathering of persons achieve the intended purpose. It is through time spent in preplanning that he can best guarantee a profitable meeting.

1. Who Is a Leader?

Leaders could be identified by including here a long list of the characteristics of effective leadership. These lists

usually sound impossible, and discouragement is not our purpose. The writer does not believe that only certain persons,
by virtue of basic inborn personality traits, are destined to
be leaders. Neither does he believe that a long inventory of
personal traits (such as ambition, creativity, initiative, neat-
ness, courage, and a high I.Q.) which can be measured in
psychological tests can guarantee that a person is a leader.
Nor does a person necessarily develop these traits through
some formalized program where a master leader checks off
each of the ingredients as the embryo leader becomes
"trained." Leadership is functional. Whether or not a person
becomes a leader depends mainly upon the requirements of
the situation in which he finds himself.

Leadership is a situational matter. A leader is a person
working in a situation where other members of the group
see him as helping them to accomplish their goals. It
is mainly by guiding in the activities of the group and demon-
strating his ability to get others to cooperate in accomplishing some task that a person truly becomes a leader.
This functional approach to leadership puts the focus on
what the leader does, not on what he is.

2. Leadership Actions

The actions or functions of any established group can usually be classified under two categories: (1) getting the tasks
of the group accomplished; and (2) maintaining the group
so that it functions well. A church-elected leader is recommended for each unit of organization to assure that these
actions are consciously and conscientiously performed.
Other officers are recommended to help share these responsibilities. Even though all the members may exert some
leadership in helping the group reach its goals, a designated
leader is usually necessary in most organizations to serve
as a backstop. There must be a guarantee that someone will
fill the gap which can be expected to appear now and then,
and accomplish the needed actions.

There is assigned to the president or the union leader—
church-elected leaders for Adult unions—the responsibil-

ity for accomplishing the two main categories of leadership functions or actions: (1) group *goal* actions, and (2) group *maintenance* actions. Each of these officers is assigned duties as chief *programing* officer and as chief *administrative* officer for the union. The leadership actions of these officers can be described in seven statements:

(1) The leader should feel *spiritually responsible* for the progress of the union and of each member. He must see his office as one to which he is *called*. He should be able to feel that he is doing what God wills for him—to say, with Jesus, "To this end was I born" (John 18:37). "But for this cause came I unto this hour" (John 12:27). He, too, should bring "forth his fruit in his season" (Psalm 1:3). Fulfilling the responsibilities of this job is a high Christian calling. It is a challenge which must be accepted spiritually, depending upon the guidance and help of the Holy Spirit, whose help will be enlisted continually through prayer.

(2) The effective leader will *stimulate* the group to action. He will initiate things which need to be done and which are not started by members. He will get things going toward the group's goal.

(3) The effective leader will *influence* the work of the group. He will direct the group and keep it on the track toward its goal.

(4) The effective leader will *inform* the group. He will be the chief source of information in many cases. He will contribute information which represents the church's point of view.

(5) The effective leader will *love* the group. He will hold the group together by encouraging members to contribute opinions and work on tasks. He will be responsible for creating a climate which is conducive to sharing ideas, learning, and training.

(6) The effective leader will *evaluate* by helping the group to judge its decisions and accomplishments—to measure progress and growth.

(7) The effective leader will *relate* to other church program organizations and to the total church ministry.

In all of the actions or functions listed, the leader will lead best as he secures involvement by union members in accomplishing these jobs. His concern will be to help potential leaders gradually develop skills by assuming leadership roles.

3. Concepts for a Learning Leader

If a president (or union leader) or group captain (or study leader) is to effectively perform the first general function in the learning group (which is the union), he should be familiar with at least a few educational theories concerning how adults learn best. There are a number of books and other sources which can be used by these leaders to gain such concepts.

(1) Learning Depends upon Motivation

Motivation determines not only how much is learned, but what is learned.

Adults are more problem-centered than subject-centered in learning motivation. Learning should mean finding answers to questions.

(2) Learning Involves Change

Adults resist change.

It is easier to learn the new than to unlearn the old.

Adults have more difficulty here because they have learned more and have more "old" learning.

(3) Learning Depends upon Capacity

Learners are not equal in capacity.

Capacity can be stretched; it can be enlarged.

The more one learns, the more he wants to learn, and the easier it becomes to learn.

(4) Learning Depends upon Previous Experience

This proposition is magnified by the function of age.

Adults have the advantage here because they possess the priceless ingredient of experience not known by youth.

(5) Learning Depends upon Perceiving Personal Relationships

Goals or problem-solving should become personal.

Adults ask, "Is this relevant to me?" "to the group?"

(6) Learning Depends upon Active Search for Meaning

Rote memorization is not satisfactory to adults.

Adults demand to know more than facts; they ask, "What does it mean?"

(7) *Learning Depends upon Feedback*

Evaluation of progress satisfies an adult's need to feel a sense of accomplishment.

An individual learns more, according to many educational tests, when he sees what and how much he is learning.

Evaluation is to be used for motivation—not as a threat or punishment by embarrassment.

(8) *Learning Depends upon Satisfactory Social and Personal Adjustment in the Learning Situation*

The group problem or goal to be achieved should be commonly accepted.

Fellowship helps create an atmosphere for learning. When a group of learners become a "group," accepting one another, understanding one another, "allowing for" one another, appreciating one another, loving one another, then a dynamic atmosphere is created which helps each member to learn more—not always *faster*, but *better* in most cases on most subjects.

(9) *Learning Is Made Possible and Powerful by the Holy Spirit*

The Holy Spirit is:

The source of truth in the world (1 John 2:27; 4:6; 5:6; John 14:17)

The Christian's teacher (Luke 12:12; 1 Cor. 2:13; John 14:26)

The Christian's challenger (Rom. 8:11,14; Gal. 4:6; John 16:7–8)

The Christian's guide (John 16:13; Acts 1:8)

The Christian's comforter (John 14:16; 15:26)

The means of God's power being felt in and through Christians as individuals and as a group (Luke 24:49; 1 John 4:13).

4. Checklist for Leaders

One of the implications of all leadership studies is that leadership can be learned. This gives encouragement and makes relevant the study of this subject by all union members. The functional definition and approach to leadership described in this chapter emphasizes the role of training in a church. Training for leadership is best accomplished in a leadership training laboratory or on-the-job training. This laboratory has been described earlier as being in operation in every Adult union. This training ground does not "turn out" persons bearing the label "leader." Leadership training requires a slower process where contributions of many Christian growth items can be assimilated.

Dr. Winston Crawley commented about leader training:

As with missionaries, we often find ourselves wishing there could be some quick shortcut to mature leadership—some machine on which specifications might be punched and the needed leader cranked out. Experience shows that leaders grow through a spiritual process which cannot be fully controlled and which is difficult to hasten.[3]

Although the process of leadership training cannot be reduced to a technical skill which can be measured precisely, there are indications in the behavior of the group which show favorable symptoms in its leadership. The following rating scale is offered to help presidents and union leaders in this evaluation.

Rating Scale for Favorable Symptoms in Leadership
(Score 5 for each item.)

( ) All members participate with a degree of regularity.
( ) Members address me no more formally than others in the group.
( ) Members frequently express real feelings.
( ) The group tends to start itself at the beginning of each meeting.
( ) Sometimes, members openly disagree with me.
( ) Members address their remarks to each other rather than to me.
( ) The group has a tendency to want to remain after time to adjourn.
( ) The group makes decisions without depending upon me as the final judge.
( ) Members seem to know what they are trying to achieve.
( ) Members speak up without asking for my permission.

[3] Winston Crawley, "Christian Maturity in the Orient," *Foreign Missions Bulletin,* Department of Missionary Education and Promotion, Foreign Mission Board, The Southern Baptist Convention, Richmond, Virginia, July, 1965.

(   ) Members do not count on me alone to handle "problem members."
(   ) "Bright ideas" originate with many members of the group.
(   ) Different individuals frequently lead the group's thinking, discussion, and procedure.
(   ) Members seem to listen to each other without interrupting, often accepting new insights and information.
(   ) Conflicts and disagreements frequently arise, but the members try to understand their nature and deal with them.
(   ) There are other members who could handle my job.
(   ) There is an absence of hostility toward me.
(   ) Members draw out and question each other to better understand their contributions.
(   ) There are evidences of spiritual growth by members.
(   ) I pray regularly for members and for the help of the Holy Spirit as I lead.

Total Score _____   Possible Score 100

IV. SELF-DIRECTED TRAINING APPROACHES

Although most of the effective church member and leader training will be offered in meetings, there are possibilities for individuals to engage in a measure of such training without attending meetings. Several personal training activities can be suggested.

1. *Personal Training Activities*

Church members who cannot attend on Sunday nights, because of the limitations of health or requirements of a vocation, can profit from studying the quarterlies.

The resource materials in the personal training guides are rich in content treatment of subjects needed for comprehensive Christian growth, membership study, and basic leadership training. The curriculum supplements and training aids (programed tests, charts, graph analyses, and picture interpretations) lend themselves well to private application. Special book reviews in these personal training guides include outlines and suggestions for individual study. These quarterlies are prepared with the intent that they be adaptable to personal training activities.

Assignments for applying the lessons in follow-through actions can be exercised by the individual upon his own initiative for meaningful and satisfying use of his training.

Church members who are able to participate in the Sunday School or other church program organizations which use the Life and Work Curriculum, will find studying the Training Union quarterlies in this curriculum especially beneficial. Since these materials are so closely correlated, a participant in one organization will need to study the corresponding units from the other organization to fully understand and apply either.

Comprehensive use of the Church Study Course includes completion of books by individuals in home study. These can be chosen for specialized leader training, or they can be selected from the suggested list of approved books for deepening and furthering the study of certain units which were begun in the lesson course quarterlies.

The Training Union Lesson Course Study Plan in the Church Study Course relates units and books appropriately and makes possible the earning of further award credits. Requirements are stated in the quarterlies.

Certain sections of the material for church leader training materials may be studied at home by individuals who qualify for such training. Even when they cannot attend on Sunday nights, these church members can perhaps participate in the training sessions which meet at other times.

These personal training activity suggestions are appropriate also for union members who do attend training meetings. Such approaches can be followed by those who wish to expand their training opportunities and to gain deeper insights into study content areas.

2. *Relating to Church Training Program*

It is suggested that Adult departments and unions can perform an extension of their training ministry by enlisting church members who cannot attend meetings on Sunday nights. Associate directors and vice-presidents or enlistment leaders can compile a special list of such prospects. They should lead efforts to secure a commitment from such individuals to join in their fellowship of study from the quarterlies and other resource materials. These materials will be distributed periodically, along with information on other training meeting opportunities in which such individuals may engage.

All individuals engaged in self-directed training should relate to the department or union to which they would belong if they were able to attend Sunday night meetings. This relation will include items discussed in the previous paragraph. It will also include invitations to participate in social and fellowship occasions, along with active members and associate members who work with younger age groups in Training Union and thus cannot attend Sunday night meetings of the union.

Personal contact of individuals for enlistment in self-directed training activities may not always be feasible. Some individuals may react against relating to a specific union or department (because of having their names on a roll or list, or for some other reason). In such cases a general mail-out of quarterlies and other training materials and information to all such adult church members would be appropriate and profitable—both for the individuals and for the church which needs trained members.

CHAPTER 8

8

Evaluating Training of Adults
Is Productive

EVALUATION is necessary in the training process. However, it is not generally utilized in the programs of education in our churches. Failure to evaluate may indicate a fear that it will reveal an embarrassing lack of accomplishment. However, evaluation should not be seen as a negative test designed simply to discover inadequacies. Adults can gain satisfaction through evaluation since it reveals accomplishments as well as areas that need improvement. For continued motivation, the adult learner must realize that he is getting somewhere in the training process. Thus, evaluation can be approached as a productive element in training.

I. What Is Evaluation?

Evaluation is a continuing fact of life. Most people are continuously evaluating the effectiveness of their own activities. They do this in an informal way as they participate in those activities. As a recipe is being followed, women taste to determine whether too much or too little spice has been added. One last time before going out, women check to see if the correct amount and shade of makeup has been applied. Men wonder, *Did I perform that introduction as effectively as I should have?*

1. Purpose and Definition

"Evaluation is a process of trying to find out whether certain actions have led to desired consequences. Ordinarily, one must (1) specify the desired consequences or outcomes of the action; (2) devise ways of measuring the degree to which the goals have been achieved; (3) carry out the action; (4) collect the desired information; and (5) make analysis and interpretation of it before going on to plan the next relevant activity." [1]

Concerning a church educating through its organizations: "An organization should be evaluated on the basis of the help it gives the church in functioning successfully." [2]

2. *Limiting Factors*

Determining how to evaluate Christian training is difficult because it concerns many intangible qualities—qualities which are difficult to measure. Any teacher knows how puzzling it is to find out what his teaching is accomplishing. Evaluating training is even more difficult.

One special difficulty is that the outcomes of training for better group behavior are fairly complex and—initially at least—not very clear to planners. . . . What kinds of attitude change can we expect from people after they experience a series of role-played episodes? Can one ever really define what it is that makes for effective group membership, or specify what skills . . . a chairman needs? [3]

Examining the behavior of people is another limiting factor in evaluating training. This can cause the members involved in a training program to feel threatened. Thus, attempts to measure how much has been accomplished in the training process seem to discourage evaluation.

Evaluation can be done at the end of an activity, but it should not be limited to this position. The first step in the evaluation process is the identification of the outcomes which the training program is to produce. This step should come during the planning. When it does not take place during the planning, another limiting factor is introduced.

----

[1] Matthew B. Miles, *Learning to Work in Groups* (New York: Bureau of Publications, Teachers' College of Columbia University, 1959), pp. 223–24. Used by permission.

[2] Howse and Thomason, *A Church Organized and Functioning* (Nashville: Convention Press, 1963), p. 17.

[3] Miles, *op. cit.*, p. 228.

It is difficult to test objectively for some of the desired outcomes because this process involves finding out what facts mean to a person or what he is doing with those facts to change his life and the lives of others. It is not enough to find out how much factual information he has. However, there are general ways of testing a program of Christian education in which a person is involved.

3. *Areas or Kinds of Evaluation*

People or groups who stop to look directly at themselves and their progress toward a goal increase their ability to move directly toward and to achieve that goal. Dangerous when overused or misused, evaluation is nevertheless an essential element in learning.[4]

There are at least four areas or kinds of evaluation for consideration in this training program. These may be used at different times in any sequence. Or, evaluation may take place in all of these areas at once.

(1) *Evaluation in regard to aim.*—This is basic evaluation, since proper evaluation presupposes a setting of objectives, goals, and aims before planning begins. Evaluating the aim helps to relate everything in the learning experiences in terms of this learning or training objective. It can help learners to relate parts to the whole and the whole to the aim. One caution should be given in this area—too much evaluating of the *aim* can cause the concept to become meaningless.

Some suggested approaches for accomplishing this evaluation are described later in this chapter under "Other Instruments."

(2) *Evaluation in regard to content.*—It is profitable for a group to stop occasionally in the training process to state exactly what has been learned. This summarizing helps members to organize their thinking and to clear up fuzzy concepts. It also helps to stimulate the learners by giving them the satisfaction of realizing that something has been

---

[4] Sara Little, *Learning Together in the Christian Fellowship* (Richmond: John Knox Press, 1956), p. 57. Used by permission.

achieved—that something has been learned. A caution needs to be offered at this point. Groups should not be forced to try to write down everything that has been learned. Some concepts cannot be committed to words.

The most commonly and traditionally used instruments for evaluating content gained are tests (such as multiple choice, true-false, filling in blanks, etc.). Described later in this chapter are pretesting and post-testing with comparison of results and writing a narrative or summary statement.

(3) *Evaluation in regard to group processes.*—This evaluation should be accomplished to help all members recognize responsibility for what the group does and develop skills as group participants. A danger exists in overemphasizing the concept of the group or "group dynamics." The process of group interaction can become so fascinating that attention is given more to the process than to the learning which is to be achieved through it.

The flow chart, (p. 135) is an intriguing instrument which can be used to evaluate the group process of participation. The Assignment Register (p. 137), though less sophisticated, is another such instrument. Group discussion and tape recordings are also effective tools.

(4) *Evaluation in regard to changes in persons.*—This area of evaluation is especially important in the context of a church training fellowship. People learn to help one another and to draw thrilling satisfaction from personal growth and from recognizing growth in others. This is the bonus which comes from Christians learning together; they are aided by the catalyst of Christian love and mutual helpfulness. A danger in this area of evaluation occurs when it is used too early for some group members or if it is used too often. When necessary questions become personal, the adult learner hesitates to reveal himself or damage his "image."

Personal testimonies can be effective instruments in evaluating changes in persons. Observation of all desired changes cannot be made by planning and evaluating teams of the union. Case studies and picture interpretation, as described later in the chapter, are also helpful tools for revealing changed attitudes as well as probable action patterns. Role playing and interpretation are also very revealing.

II. VALUES OF EVALUATION

Evaluation is a necessary element in training if the leader is to find out whether certain planned actions have led to desired consequences. There are other values to be received in measuring the degree to which goals have been achieved.

1. Satisfaction in Gains

Evaluation not only shows whether and to what degree aims have been achieved or desired consequences accomplished, but it also gives the learner himself a strong degree of satisfaction. He is pleased when he realizes that he has accomplished something, that in the learning process he has progressed from what he knew or where he was to what he knows or where he is now.

This element, missing in so many learning situations because evaluation is not exercised, can also be credited with much of the dissatisfaction and termination of participation in learning groups by many adults. The adult is not generally expected by this society to be a "learner." He is recognized first as a "producer" or "doer." He does not have the social pressures to engage in learning as youth do. The adult must obtain some joy and satisfaction sufficient to motivate him in learning activities. Even as he requires that learning goals and content be relevant to his problems or needs, he also requires the knowledge that he is making progress toward those goals. The adult will not continue training indefinitely without knowing definitely what he is training to do, and without having a measurable point of achievement.

2. Direction for Effort

Evaluation is also profitable to the leader because it indicates through what has been measured, the direction and kinds of effort needed in future training. New goals or objectives can be set, based upon those which have been achieved, in total or in part.

Evaluation of past performance not only indicates the direction of effort, but also makes possible the estimating of a schedule or timetable for certain future learning events. This is most helpful in a day when the calendar and the clock become dictators of people's activities.

III. Tools for Evaluation

There are some tools and instruments of measurement which can be used in evaluating this training organization.

1. Record System

Adults are creatures of habit. In his book *The Improvement of Teaching in the Sunday School,* Gaines S. Dobbins has written that habits of members of the Sunday School can be measured by observing the record system. He added: "Life consists largely of habitual ways of behaving. A habit is a regular way of thinking, feeling, or acting, that has become more or less automatic through repetition." [5]

As a means of accomplishing the objective of training to perform the responsibilities of church members, eight habits have been grouped together and assigned percentage values. These habits, which are felt to be essential in church member development, form the "Eight Point Record System." These habits can be observed and recorded. Although the quality of the results gained from following these habits is not expected to be measured, all of the points are judged to have positive values. They do record the measure of success or failure with which the habits are being formed. As these habits become permanent, it is certain that the individual will have his life enriched and will be better able to live and serve in his church as God and his fellow church members have the right to expect.

No valid figures for purposes of measurement or comparison have been compiled on a scale large enough to give a

[5] Nashville: The Sunday School Board of the Southern Baptist Convention, 1943, p. 152.

true picture of what adults are doing. However, the figures which are entered on the Eight Point Record System do offer a valuable measure of the church membership training being done by individuals in a church. Compilations of these figures are used to disclose much of analytical value concerning the program of training being given in a particular union, department, or in the entire Training Union.

(1) *Values of records.*—What are the values of records?

First, the eight points are used to lead each member to do certain practical things which will help him in church member training. Checking the record helps a member to check on himself.

Second, the tabulation of the records helps those responsible for directing various phases of the work in a union to know which items of training need to be given attention. Thus, they promote purposeful activity directed toward needs. The Adult learner is problem-centered in his learning motivation. He responds to learning opportunities which are directed toward his felt needs or problems. Records can help those who are responsible for planning to focus on problem areas.

Records, then, serve to reveal a measure of achievement. They indicate to some degree what is being accomplished in the lives of union members. One writer has advanced the theory that one reason for an emphasis upon records is the "realization of the need of recognition of achievement." [6] There is a deep-seated desire for recognition in the individual personality.

Accurately kept records can reveal progress, success, and failure. They can also stimulate to action. They indicate what is being done and they guide in planning new action goals. Motivation can come from the study of records. It is for these reasons that every enterprise, regardless of its nature or purpose, uses records.

(2) *Interpretation of Eight Point Record System.*—Consider the following:

---

[6] J. Clark Hensley, *The Pastor As Educational Director* (Kansas City: Central Seminary Press, 1946), p. 71.

Present.—A member qualifies on this point if he is present in the weekly meeting of his union or is sent to some other church to do Training Union work. The evaluation is 10 percent.

On Time.—A member checks "On Time" if he is in the meeting room at the announced time for the weekly meeting. If an opening assembly precedes the union meeting, this means in the meeting place of this assembly. The evaluation is 10 percent.

Studied Lesson.—"Studied Lesson" is checked if the member reads in advance of each session the "Material for Study" in the quarterly or some other designated material. The evaluation is 15 percent.

On Program.—To qualify on this point, a member must participate in the sessions as often as his group has that responsibility. (If a group or study leader is assigned to lead an entire unit of several sessions, this point's interpretation would have to be changed to say: A member must participate in the unit study and accept at least one assignment from the group captain or study leader during each month.) He should not read his assignment from the quarterly, but he should use the opportunity for self-expression based on study resources for the subject being discussed. The evaluation is 15 percent.

Study Course.—"Study Course" is checked by a member if he has completed a study of at least one textbook in the Church Study Course during the past twelve months. The evaluation is 10 percent.

Daily Bible Reading.—A member is qualified to check this point if he has followed daily the Bible Readers' Course for the previous week. The evaluation is 15 percent.

Attending Preaching.—To make the grade on "Attending Preaching," a member must attend the evening preaching service in the church where he holds membership. An exception is allowed when he is away from his own church as a representative of the Training Union or when his church does not have such a service. The evaluation is 10 percent.

Giving.—To qualify on this point, a member must give, systematically, into his church treasury according to the church plan. The evaluation is 15 percent.

2. Standards of Excellence

The Standard of Excellence for an Adult union is a training guide. Its purpose is to define and outline a program of work for training church members. Since evaluation has been defined as measuring progress toward a goal, it must be preceded by the planning of goals and a program of training activities for reaching them. The Standard of Excellence, then, becomes both a planning guide and an instrument for evaluation.

The Adult union Standard of Excellence includes the items which an Adult union should be practicing if it is to accomplish its goals. An Adult union aims to provide training in the various areas needed by one who is to be an effective, growing, serving church member. The Standard itself is not to be thought of as a goal; it is more nearly a set of working drawings for building a program which functions toward the achieving of its assigned training goals.

Complete statements of the Standards of Excellence for unions using the regular and the alternate plans of organization, as well as a Standard for an Adult department, are included as Appendix I of this book. A careful check of the sections will reveal the balanced curriculum which it outlines—items which are related to the tasks assigned Training Union and to the needs of growing Adult church members.

3. *Other Instruments*

In addition to the sort of evaluation that goes on continuously in the mind of a good leader, there are more definite approaches to evaluating which also can be used.

An *observer* watches union activities objectively and analytically, then reports and leads the group to see itself as he saw them. He evaluates member performance and achievement of stated goals or aims.

Group discussion depends upon a skilful leader. The leader must establish a climate of full expression. Frequently, this can be done by dividing members into buzz groups and having recorders report comments. Group discussion can reveal emotional satisfactions, increase in self-esteem, personality growth, and human relations skills of members.

Tape recordings can provide accurate information, especially of group discussion, which may be used for evaluation in union or department sessions.

A *flow chart* can indicate the degree to which members have participated in a discussion. It can also reveal possible leader domination. If the chart is properly kept, it will indicate who talks to whom and whether some members monopolize the discussion while others have no opportunity to speak or withdraw.

In the flow chart below, comments made to the group as a whole are indicated by arrows which point only to the middle of the circle. Arrows with points on both ends indicate that statements were made to individuals who, in turn, responded. Short lines crossing one end of the double arrows identify the person initiating the exchange.

A "bunching" of arrows in this chart shows that one person had more comments directed toward him and made more responses than any other two members, while one member made no verbal contribution to the group effort at problem-solving. Some possible side-issue conversation is also indicated.

Displaying the chart to the group at a later date, without

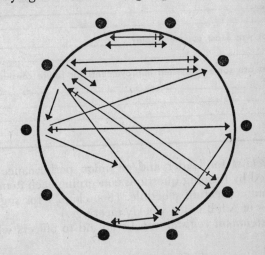

identifying members, can serve to correct discussion participation problems without embarrassment to individuals.

Reaction sheets can be used by observers, but they can
be used more effectively by group members in postmeeting
evaluation. Upon adjournment, the sheets would be turned
in unsigned to be used by the planning team and the leader
for improving future sessions.

Questions on the sheets can be either detailed or simply-
stated guides, such as the following:

What do you think was the aim? _____
_____
_____

Was it accomplished? ___Yes ___Partially ___Not at all
Why? (Explain) _____
_____
_____
_____

What were the best features or most commendable activities
of the session? _____
_____
_____

What was least commendable? _____
_____

What are some suggested improvements for future consideration? _____
_____
_____

A *checklist* for leader and/or union performance could
be devised by forming questions concerning each item listed
on the union meeting schedule. (See chap. 7 for suggested
schedules of Adult union weekly meetings.)

An *assignment register* can be an aid to officers who are

responsible for involving all union members in union activities. The president or union leader, along with other officers, could make a frequent review of such a register. This would be especially helpful in unions using the alternate organization plan.

A possible arrangement of such a register is offered here.

ASSIGNMENT REGISTER				
Member	Type Assignment	Date Assigned	By (Officer)	Performed?

Picture interpretation involves displaying a scene and asking members to point out right and/or wrong actions. Or, members may be shown a simple picture which they are to use in constructing a human conflict situation. Later changes in attitudes or action patterns can be revealed as they offer solutions. *Role play* and *drama* also can be used effectively for such evaluations.

Rating sheets may be used. Each member ranks union activities or training features according to a rating scale.

Comparing results of tests given before and after a study can be helpful.

Members may be asked to write *narratives* describing what they have learned or summary statements which express the central thought conveyed during a session.

Case studies may be used effectively. Members may be

asked to note right and wrong practices. Or, case studies can present problems followed by alternate solutions which the members rank as proper or effective action. Recording case studies often adds effectiveness.

IV. MORE ADEQUATE CRITERIA FOR EVALUATING

That there should be more adequate means for evaluating the training program is emphasized when one thinks of a rather common illustration relating to education. Many times at the end of the day a parent will ask his child, "Well, what did you learn in school today?" The child's reply might be that he had learned to spell some new words; that Indians lived in this land when white men first came; or some new concept in mathematics. These things he could recognize as facts which he had been taught.

In a child's school day, who could say what was truly learned—either in quantity or content? How can it be enumerated what the child has learned by way of patience through problem-solving in mathematics; of meanings in words spelled; of attitudes planted concerning other racial groups in this country; of appreciation for discipline and authority as exercised by the teacher; or of the ability to make friends and adjust to the group?

It seems that many adults have difficulty when asked to comment upon what they are "getting from" Training Union. They are apt to recognize only the more obvious facts which may be remembered from units studied or specific skills practiced during some activity.

1. Changed Lives

Reflecting the tasks of Training Union

The basic purpose of Training Union has been described as training church members to work together skilfully in conducting a church's basic work. In evaluating a church's program of training adults one would need to ask, How are Adult church members improving in knowledge, skills, and action patterns relating to these tasks or to their church's essential work? This process is difficult to conceive. The following questions, grouped according to Training Union *tasks*, should help in an important and ultimate area of evaluation—changes in the lives and work of participant church members.

(1) *Teach systematic theology.*—How much greater has the depth of understanding and conviction concerning theology or New Testament doctrines become in those who have participated in the program of Training Union work?

How well and how often do members interpret their beliefs to others?

What books are being studied on Baptist theology and on the theology of other faiths?

(2) *Teach Christian ethics.*—By what method can the impact of more consistent Christian character—as concerns language, Lord's Day observance, honesty, alcohol education, moral conduct, social practices, civic righteousness—be evaluated?

Are more homes realizing the heights of divinely intended joy in family worship, problem-solving, recreation, and other training in Christian living?

How many pastors, ministers of education and music, missionaries, and other vocational Christian workers gained their first insight of a call to service through exercising the responsibilities of an office or studying resource materials in a Training Union?

How many more Christians, even adults, are recognizing and answering God's call to church vocations?

How many Christians, because of spiritual perceptiveness and understanding gained through training, are being used to help others become aware of and respond to such calls? Larger percentages of new seminary students give testimony to the role of Training Union in revealing their call than to that of any other agency.

(3) *Teach Christian history*—What convictions for current action have been developed in studies of our Baptist heritage provided uniquely by Training Union?

How much more alert to encroachments on religious liberty today are church members who have gained appreciations for the role of their Baptist forebears in securing this freedom for all?

What guidance has been gained from lessons of the past by Baptists now in responsible positions of leadership, both in government and denominational life?

(4) *Teach church polity and organization.*—How many church members have learned to understand the work and governing covenant relationships of a New Testament church through resource studies in Training Union?

Where can the next generation of deacons and other adult church officers gain the experience and skills in presiding over business and planning meetings?

When do most church members first learn to exercise a voice in electing officers and otherwise governing themselves in a small organizational unit within the spiritual democracy of a church?

What can the study of other forms of church government contribute to the practical understanding and exercise of our own unique congregational concept?

(5) *Give orientation to new church members.*—What is the measure of active Christian testimony which has been conserved in the lives of new church members who have had fellowship with more mature Christians in the training program of their churches?

How much needed service will be rendered by new members who have been adequately oriented into the full church program of Christian growth and member training?

What future doubts have been settled due to adequate counseling of new Christians concerning the meaning of the salvation experience and church membership?

(6) *Train all church members to worship, witness, learn, and minister daily.*—Has training established for a substantial number of Baptists the habit of daily prayer and Bible reading?

What increased strength has come to those committed in the Training Union to practicing a consistent devotional life of personal Bible reading and prayer? W. L. Howse has related that during his more than twenty years of teaching at Southwestern Baptist Theological Seminary, he repeatedly asked classes of students where their definite interest in Bible reading had begun. He said:

The majority have always paid tribute to the Training Union as the influence which prompted interest in the daily reading and study of God's Word. Daily prayer, so essential to Christian growth, is facilitated through daily reading of the Scriptures.[7]

What measure of better churchmanship is practiced by trained church members?

Do more Baptists who have been influenced by the church training program attend all preaching services and prayer meetings?

Is more visiting done for the church because members have been trained in a practical laboratory in how to visit?

In what number are to be found converts and strengthened Christians as a result of training given church members in performing the function of witnessing?

How much more is given for the work of Christ through his churches because of the acceptance of stewardship joys and responsibilities by those trained in Training Union?

How many more tithers have been enlisted because of those trained to share the doctrine of stewardship and enlist others in its practice? One successful pastor has commented: "The adults underwrite our financial program. . . . They give freely, gladly, and regularly when they are enlisted and taught the joy of tithing and systematic giving." [8]

How many more persons have been won to Christ? How many members have been added to the churches by baptism through the efforts of trained church members? How many have developed concern for the lost?

What is the measure of heightened missionary endeavors which have come through the efforts, or with the support, of those who have had their compassion sensitized and their

[7] "With You—If You Teach Them to Observe," *The Baptist Training Union Magazine*, December, 1952, p. 9.

[8] Ramsey Pollard, "Adults Underwrite Our Whole Church Program," *The Sunday School Builder*, November, 1949, p. 52.

vision lifted to feel and see spiritual needs outside their own churches? The Foreign Mission Board rates the Training Union as one of its most effective avenues of missionary education. The secretary for education and promotion has related as an example the recommendation in one Training Union adult quarterly of a certain pamphlet as being available from the Foreign Mission Board. He said that "182,000 requests came to us." This indicates "the interest Training Union members develop for Foreign Missions and foretells of the impact a knowledge of Foreign Missions received in a Training Union will have upon them." [8]

What have been the results as men and women have first learned to express themselves on spiritual matters in the conducive surroundings of a congenial group of fellow Christians in Training Union, then to find themselves able to give expression or testimony in groups outside the church which need a Christian witness?

(7) *Train leaders for the church and the denomination.*— How many more people have first taken some degree of responsibility in Training Union, later to take on participant roles in the total ministry of the church? J. Howard Williams, late president of Southwestern Baptist Theological Seminary, testified: "The 'B.Y.P.U.' meant much to me because it afforded an opportunity for experience. . . . it was more or less the beginning of my growth in grace, and certainly in active service." [9]

What self-expression skills have been developed in Baptists because of participant experiences given in the regular program of work in Training Union? Eugene L. Hill has told how the Lord called him to preach while he was taking part on a B.Y.P.U. program. Dr. Hill went on to say: "Practically all of the 'speech training' I ever got was in Training Union, and most of my early knowledge of Bible

---

[8] Eugene L. Hill, Richmond, Virginia, in a letter to Forrest Feezor, September 26, 1957.

[9] J. Howard Williams, in personal letter to Forrest Feezor, September 24, 1957.

doctrine, stewardship, and church membership responsibility was gained in Training Union." [10]

Where are the men and women who, having been responsible for the duties of an office or committee and having directed others in planning and reporting concerning phases of the work, have developed basic leadership skills?

How many leaders of other age groups and general officers, both in Training Union and throughout all of the organizations of the churches and associations, gained their basic training in an adult union?

How many more potential leaders will be discovered by union and department officers now charged with this definite responsibility?

What size reservoir of informed and growing leaders and administrators will be produced through the new program of recruitment and leader training in Training Union?

(8) *Provide organization and leadership for special projects of the church.*—With what measure can the impact of coordinated Baptist promotion of special simultaneous events be gauged?

How much more support in planning and subscribing increasing budgets will come as Training Union trains church members to conduct them?

With what increased success will revival efforts be crowned when church members are trained to witness effectively in advance of the harvest-reaping services?

What will be the possible limit of special missions offerings when a church utilizes its total organizational resources in projects of such import?

(9) *Provide and interpret information regarding the work of the church and the denomination.*—Can constructive denominational loyalty developed through regular participation be valued highly enough in these days of uncertainty regarding other movements and allegiances?

Perhaps the statement of a consecrated layman who serves throughout his church would be a more effective statement than any professional analyst evaluating how well this or-

---

[10] Hill, *op. cit.*

ganization accomplishes its tasks. He speaks of Training Union as giving a "second wind" to his adult Christian life, saying of this church program organization:

Here we find strength through fellowship in a union; we are kept informed concerning our church and denomination; and we participate in a continuing refresher course in training for greater knowledge. We are also directed in practical activities which call upon us to use our knowledge and abilities. This enables us to continue to be useful in the work of the kingdom.[11]

2. Continuing Christian Growth

None of the inadequate questions which relate to the stated tasks of Training Union can effectively measure the merit of the program of a church training adults. They do, however, support and give substance to the premise that values have been and are being derived—values which affect the church and its mission and functions, as well as the Christian growth and skills of individual members.

The only adequate measure would have to be gauged by the standards of Christ for his followers. How much nearer participants have come and caused others to approach—in attitudes, skills, knowledge, and service—the likeness of Christ? No man can compute or judge. All must "press toward the mark for the prize of the high calling of God in Christ Jesus" (Phil. 3:14). Although it is certain that Southern Baptist programs and materials, like the lives of Southern Baptist church members, cannot attain the goal of Christlikeness, the challenge to improve must be kept alive.

The fact is that the program available for a church to train its adults has much to be desired by these standards. There is, however, within the design of the program challenging, scripturally based practical objectives and goals, well-stated tasks, excellent content, a choice of organizational vehicles, suggestions for necessary planning, and an outline of profitable meetings. These should be more than

---

[11] W. S. Bagwell, "Second Wind for Adults," *The Beacon,* First Baptist Church, Durham, North Carolina, November 8, 1956.

adequate if appropriated by a church and adults who want to accomplish the training.

And so . . .

To accomplish many of the features of a church's program of training and the goals of Training Union program tasks, a positive spirit concerning adulthood and the role of adults in society and in the churches needs to be developed. There must come a recognition that adulthood is the most joyous, productive, and fulfilling time of life. Churches must give priority to enlisting adults and providing church member and leader training for them because of their numbers, their unique needs, and their unique relationships to the other age groups and to the church. In this relationship they furnish the constituency by bringing their children, by providing the leadership, and by contributing financial and church support. To make these truths urgently clear and to enlist "disciples" to witness concerning them is a consuming need. This is where improving the program for a church training its adults must begin.

Churches are immeasurably hampered in accomplishing their mission for Christ because of untrained adult members and leaders. Churches find in the program of training their most practical hope for alleviating this hindering burden. Churches and church leaders who expect to reap the solutions to these priority needs will reasonably give priority support in providing leadership, time, and other resources, as well as by becoming personally involved in the program.

Let it be the sincere desire and earnest prayer of every reader of this book that unfolding years will find the program improving, the spirit of the adults in the churches more enthusiastic, and the service to Christ in the world heightened.

"Thou hast set [our] feet in a large room" (Psalm 31:8).

For Review and Written Work

CHAPTER 1

1. What is your definition of a church? 2. Explain briefly: A Church is an organism. 3. List four functions of a church.

CHAPTER 2

4. Define training. 5. List four of the tasks of Training Union. 6. State the maturity concept of adulthood.

CHAPTER 3

7. List the three courses of study used by Training Union. 8. Training Union Life and Work Curriculum provides two basic quarterlies for use in Adult unions. List them.

CHAPTER 4

9. Name three elements in an Adult union organization. 10. What is the value of the committee system in an Adult Union? 11. List four responsibilities of your committee, or the committee which interests you most, in an Adult union.

CHAPTER 5

12. Name the four recommended officers in the alternate organization plan. 13. Why is the study leader *selected* rather than *elected*? 14. State your opinion concerning the organization plan which will best meet the needs of your union. 15. State the purpose of an Adult department.

CHAPTER 6

16. Define planning. 17. Name the two kinds of unit planning. 18. Name three benefits of the Unit Selection Plan. 19. Which officers make up the comprehensive planning team in the regular plan? in the alternate plan? 20. List the "Guides in Planning for Learning."

CHAPTER 7

21. Define meetings. 22. Outline the suggested schedule for your union. 23. List five concepts in Adult learning needed by leaders.

CHAPTER 8

24. Define evaluation. 25. List two important values of evaluation. 26. State the purpose of the Standard of Excellence. 27. Explain: "The Only True Measure" for evaluating the program of Adult work.

Appendix

I.

Standards of Excellence
for
ADULT UNIONS USING REGULAR ORGANIZATION
ADULT UNIONS USING ALTERNATE ORGANIZATION
ADULT DEPARTMENTS

STANDARD OF EXCELLENCE
Adult Union, Baptist Training Union

I. ORGANIZATION

REGULAR PLAN

1. *Officers.*—President, vice-president, secretary, group captains, social leader, missionary leader, and Bible readers' leader. (Song leader and pianist recommended if needed.) (1) All officers shall be members of the church where they serve. (2) Each officer shall be instructed in his duties at the beginning of his term of office. (3) The president and at least four other officers shall hold, or earn during the quarter, an award on *A Church Training Adults.*

2. *Committees.*—Program, membership, social, missionary, and Bible reading. (1) The program committee shall meet each month to plan the studies for the weekly meetings. (2) The other committee chairmen shall direct the work of their committee members through *monthly committee* meetings or individual assignments.

3. *Groups.*—The union shall be divided into groups, each with a group captain.

ALTERNATE PLAN

1. *Officers.*—Union leader, enlistment leader, study leaders (as required by study units for the quarter), and activities leader. (1) All officers shall be members of the church where they serve. (2) The union leader shall be elected by the church. (3) Each officer shall be instructed in his duties at the beginning of his

147

term of office. (4) The union leader and at least two other officers shall hold, or earn during the quarter, an award on *A Church Training Adults*.

II. MEETINGS

1. *Weekly Meeting.*—The union shall conduct a weekly meeting, with study based upon Training Union lesson course materials published by the Baptist Sunday School Board. (1) Every active (Baptist) member attending shall accept some programing responsibility during each quarter.

2. *Planning Meetings.*—The officers of the union shall meet monthly to review the work of the union and make plans for the next month. (1) The union shall cooperate with the Training Union in its plan for the general planning meeting. (2) The secretary or enlistment leader shall make a written report of the work of the union for the past month. (3) The other officers shall present written plans for the coming month. (4) The president or union leader shall make a monthly written report to the department planning meeting if the department is organized; otherwise, to the Training Union council.

III. ACTIVITIES

1. *Study.*—(1) *Lesson Courses*—The union shall follow the Training Union lesson course materials published by the Baptist Sunday School Board. (2) *Church Study Course*—The union shall participate in at least one study course every twelve months, using a book of the Church Study Course of the Baptist Sunday School Board.

2. *Daily Bible Reading and Prayer.*—The union shall follow the course for individual daily Bible reading and daily prayer as outlined in one of the Baptist Adult Union quarterlies.

3. *Worship.*—(1) The union shall promote attendance upon the evening preaching service. (2) The union shall promote attendance upon the weekly prayer meeting of the church. (3) The union shall promote daily family worship in every home represented.

4. *Stewardship and Missions.*—(1) The union shall promote education in stewardship, tithing, and systematic giving by all of its members to church expenses, benevolences, and missions according to the church plan. (2) The union shall encourage the enlistment of all of its members in active service in other church organizations and activities. (3) The union shall take

part each quarter in some practical missionary or other follow-through activity. (4) Every active member shall be urged to pray for and witness to lost people daily.

5. *Social Life.*—The union shall have at least one social activity each quarter. Combination socials, held with Sunday School classes or other church organizations, may be recognized not more than twice a year as meeting this requirement.

6. *Visitation.*—Regular visitation of all absentees and prospects shall be sponsored.

IV. ACHIEVEMENT

1. The union shall encourage every member to make a high grade on the Eight Point Record System.

2. The weekly average number of members making 70 percent or above * shall be at least two-thirds of the weekly average enrolment for the quarter.**

NOTE.—*If the union has reached the points on this Standard for a quarter, application for the Standard award should be made to the state Training Union secretary on a form provided by him. To the union qualifying as Standard, the quarterly Standard award will be sent by the Baptist Sunday School Board.*

STANDARD OF EXCELLENCE

ADULT DEPARTMENT, BAPTIST TRAINING UNION

I. ORGANIZATION

1. *Officers.*—Director, associate director, secretary, song leader, and pianist, elected by the church.

The director, associate director, and secretary shall hold, or earn during the quarter, an award on *A Church Training Adults.*

2. *Grading.*—Two or more Adult unions, graded by congenial age groups.

3. *Enrolment.*—One fourth of the resident church membership, ages 25 and above, shall be enrolled as members in the Adult department, or as workers in other places in the Training Union. In churches with more than one Adult department, each department shall meet this requirement for its age span.

* Add the weekly totals of members making 70 percent or above and divide the sum by the number of Sundays in the quarter.

**Add the weekly enrolments and divide the sum by the number of Sundays in the quarter.

II. Meetings

1. *Weekly Meeting.*—(1) The department shall conduct a weekly assembly of all unions, preferably before the union meetings. (2) The department shall cooperate with the Training Union in attendance upon any general assemblies which it may hold.

2. *Department Planning Meeting.*—The department director shall hold a monthly meeting of the department officers and presidents or union leaders of unions to plan the work of the department for the coming month.

3. *Training Union General Planning Meeting.*—The department shall cooperate with the Training Union in its plan for the general planning meeting.

III. Activities

1. *Study.*—(1) *Lesson Courses*—The Adult department shall follow the lesson course in the quarterlies for Adults published by the Baptist Sunday School Board. (2) *Church Study Course.*—The Adult department, in cooperation with the plans of the Training Union, shall lead its unions to participate in at least one study course every twelve months, studying a book for Adults in the Church Study Course published by the Baptist Sunday School Board.

2. *Daily Bible Reading.*—The Adult department shall follow the Daily Bible Readers' Course for individual reading and daily devotions as published in one of the Adult union quarterlies.

3. *Worship.*—(1) The Adult department shall promote attendance upon the evening preaching service. (2) The Adult department shall promote attendance upon the church prayer meeting. (3) The Adult department shall promote daily family worship in every home represented.

4. *Stewardship and Missions.*—(1) The Adult department shall promote education in stewardship, tithing, and the enlistment of all of its members in systematic giving to church expenses, benevolences, and missions, according to the church plan. (2) The Adult department shall encourage the enlistment of all of its members in active service in other church activities and organizations. (3) The Adult department shall seek to enlist all of its active (Baptist) members in praying for and witnessing to lost people daily.

5. *Social Life.*—The Adult department shall promote a program of Christian social life as required in the Standard of the

Adult union. Once each year the unions may combine their socials into a department social.

6. *Visitation*—Regular visitation of all absentees and prospects shall be sponsored.

IV. ACHIEVEMENT

At least one half of the unions of the Adult department shall qualify as Standard unions for the quarter.

NOTE: *If the department has reached the points on this Standard for a quarter, application for the Standard award should be made to the state Training Union secretary on the form provided by him. To the department qualifying as Standard, the quarterly Standard award will be sent by the Baptist Sunday School Board.*

II.

GLOSSARY

Activity—An action, process, or performance used to achieve a goal.

Church Leader Training—A training program which includes Potential Leader Training and Specialized Leader Training.

Church Member Training—The basic continuing training for all church members.

Church Program Organization—An organization to which a church assigns responsibility for basic continuing activities.

Content Areas—The content which church members must study in order to be trained to do the work of a church. The four content areas of the Training Union are systematic theology, Christian history, Christian ethics, and church polity and organization.

Curriculum—The activities, materials, and experiences used by a church to reach its education goals.

Curriculum Materials—Educational instruments designed to help learners and leaders plan, engage in, and evaluate learning experiences.

Education—The process by which persons grow in understanding, form new attitudes, and develop actions consistent with the example of Christ.

Evaluation—The process by which progress toward a goal is measured.

Function—A basic kind of action which is consistent with the nature of the church. The four basic functions of a church are to worship, proclaim, educate, and minister.

Goal—A statement of intention to do a measurable quantity and/or quality of results by a specific time.

Lesson Course Study Plan—A provision which allows Adults in Training Union to earn Church Study Course credit for participating in designated units of study from their lesson courses.

New Member Orientation—Plans and resources for introducing new church members through counseling and classwork into the fellowship which they have joined.

Objective—A statement of a church's intention.

Organism—A living being or thing composed of functioning parts with the element of life being independent or more fundamental than the parts making up the whole.

Organization—An orderly arrangement of leaders and members in relationship to one another according to their assigned responsibilities in carrying out the program of a church.

Potential Leader Training—A training program for discovering, recruiting, and training church members who give evidence of leadership ability.

Program—A group of basic continuing activities of primary importance in moving a church toward its objectives.

Programing—The process of planning in detail a basic continuing activity.

Program Service—A basic continuing activity which churches perform to support the carrying out of program tasks.

Special Project—A short-term church activity which has a fixed beginning and ending, and supports one or more church programs.

Specialized Leader Training—A training program for leaders of church program organizations and leaders who have been assigned specific church tasks.

Task—A basic continuing activity, the performance of which is necessary to assist a church in achieving its purpose.

Training—Education in knowledge and skills through study and practice.

Unit Selection Plan—A procedure for Adult unions in which members select units for study from those in Training Union lesson course materials each quarter.